MEDIATION MATTERS

MEDIATION MATTERS

PRACTICAL NEGOTIATION STRATEGIES FROM
A NATIONALLY RECOGNIZED MEDIATOR

MICHAEL L. RUSSELL

Clovercroft Publishing

Mediation Matters: Practical Negotiation Strategies
from a Nationally Recognized Mediator

©2022 by Michael L. Russell

Published by Clovercroft Publishing, Franklin, Tennessee

Scripture taken from THE HOLY BIBLE, NEW INTERNATIONAL
VERSION®, NIV® Copyright © 1973, 1978, 1984, 2011 by Biblica, Inc.™
Used by permission. All rights reserved worldwide.

Edited by Gail Fallen

Cover Design by Suzanne Lawing

Interior Design by Suzanne Lawing

Printed in the United States of America

978-1-954437-60-9

About the Author

Michael L. Russell is a nationally recognized mediator who serves as a neutral in cases throughout the United States. His writings have been published in the *American Journal of Trial Advocacy*, the *University of Memphis Law Review*, the *Seton Hall Constitutional Law Journal*, the *Ohio Northern University Law Review*, the *Pepperdine Dispute Resolution Law Journal*, and *Employee Rights Quarterly*. He lives in Nashville with his family and their rescue dog (which they think is a pit bull terrier). This is his first book.

Visit Michael's website at
www.michaelrussellonline.com.

Dedication

For the women in my life:

Heather Russell, the perfect spouse
and life partner
and
Linda Russell, my mother,
whose sacrifices I can never repay

Contents

Introduction

After almost twenty years as a litigator, I had developed a pretty good side gig. I discovered that I had a knack for mediating cases, and word was getting out. I'm often asked, "When did you become a full-time neutral?" To tell you the truth, I don't know. I just looked at my calendar one day, and that was all I was doing. At some point, being a litigator had become the side job.

I eventually resigned from my law firm and made mediation my full-time job. Around that time, I also began writing monthly articles, which I emailed to lawyers I knew. These articles shared my thoughts on negotiation and mediation advocacy. This was my effort at shameless self-promotion. As it turned out, those monthly articles took on a life of their own. I began getting emails from lawyers across the country, asking to be put on my email list. Lawyers from New York to Los Angeles asked me if they could share my articles with their law firms.

I was flattered that my short nuggets of negotiation advice were making an impact. At some point, I decided to organize them into a book. You're now holding the product of those efforts.

The goal of this book is to make you think more deliberately about the negotiation process. I used to say that, as a litigator, I was a practitioner of conflict. Over time, I realized I was wrong. Lawyers should primarily be problem solvers, and I came to understand that most problems can be better solved through negotiation than litigation. I hope you agree, and I hope this book will help you in your efforts.

1.

Preparing Your Client

I recently received an astute question from a bright young lawyer. He was handling his first mediation without a partner accompanying him. His client, a small business, was in its first lawsuit. The owner had no experience with mediations. This lawyer said, "I've prepared myself for this mediation, but how should I prepare my client?"

Lawyers often come to mediations with clients who are sophisticated negotiators in their own right. Other times, however, this may be their first rodeo. With rare exceptions, neither plaintiffs nor small businesses look for opportunities to dive into litigation. As one of my mediator colleagues is fond of saying, "Litigation is not the way sane people want to spend their time."

Here were my thoughts on preparing clients who find themselves in a mediation for the first time:

- Make sure they understand the process. Some call it "shuttle diplomacy." Others say mediations are similar to buying a used car. Make sure your client understands this. I'm surprised how many people come to mediations thinking they will spend the day in the same room with the opposing party.

- Explain the difference between a "goal" and a "bottom line." It's perfectly fine to come to the mediation with a goal. This means you have prepared for the mediation, reviewed strengths and weaknesses, and have an idea where you would like to steer the negotiation. By contrast, a bottom line might mean your client is coming to the mediation inflexible and unwilling to listen. The beauty of a mediation is that people are willing to agree to things at the end of the mediation that they were not willing to agree to at the beginning. Having a bottom line at the beginning of the mediation defeats the purpose of the process.

- Remind your client what happens if there's no settlement. Too often in negotiations, the perfect becomes the enemy of the good. People are tempted to walk away from a good deal because they are focused on a perfect deal. I try to redirect litigants' attention from the "perfect deal" to the "real world." There may be years of litigation. There will be significant expense. There will be intrusive discovery. There will be a disruptive trial. There may be lengthy appeals. The alternative to a good deal is not a perfect deal. The alternative to a good deal is much wasted time and money.

- Remind your client what Abraham Lincoln said. Lincoln, the trial lawyer, once told his fellow attorneys: "Discourage litigation. Persuade your neighbors to compromise whenever you can. Point out to them how the nominal winner is often the real loser—in fees, expenses, and waste of time."[1]

2.

Explain the "Game" to Your Client

In every mediation, I spend a portion of the introductory remarks explaining the mediation process to the parties. I take special care to do this if I think that one of the parties is not a very sophisticated negotiator or comes from a cultural background that makes the mediation process foreign to them. In other words, I explain the "game." I tell them that, statistically, there is a very high success rate in all mediations. I explain to them the concept of shuttle diplomacy. I acknowledge that the lawyers will call this process shuttle diplomacy, but it looks an awful lot like what happens when someone buys a used car.

Nevertheless, I am occasionally surprised when a party gets frustrated early on in the mediation when the other side will not simply cut to the chase. I have been in more than one mediation where a party gets frustrated at both the mediator and their lawyer for what they perceive is dragging out the mediation process.

For example, I have a colleague who is an excellent mediator in another city. He recently told me about a mediation involving international parties. Some of these parties were very unfamiliar with the American mediation process. Those parties grew increasingly frustrated with the mediator, the process, and their own counsel when everyone insisted on taking part in the customary give and take of mediation.

They didn't know the game.

I personally believe that the mediation process is very valuable. While it may seem odd to make a series of offers and counteroffers, this game enables litigants to reach settlements and avoid courtrooms on a regular basis. I think it is one of the best things to happen in civil litigation. There is an element of early gamesmanship in mediations. It's the idea of starting high—or low—and working toward some compromise in the middle. It's part of the process. For parties who are unfamiliar with it, it is incumbent upon attorneys to explain this process in advance of the mediation.

3.

Who Should Participate in Mediation?

One of the most important decisions we face is who should participate in a mediation. Effective lawyers give careful consideration to this when preparing for the negotiation.

In the book *Designing Systems and Processes for Managing Disputes*, the authors write about the importance of "social capital" in negotiations: "People within these positive social networks will be more likely to trust each other. . . . They also more often trust the acquaintances of those within their social networks. Further, in positive social networks, reputations spread quickly, acting as a deterrent to dishonest actions within negotiations."[1]

In other words, when opposing parties in a negotiation have social capital that can be spent in the negotiation, research suggests that a settlement becomes more likely. In a business dispute with multiple investors, for example, it is often better if the lead negotiators have mutual respect for one another. In an employment discrimination case, it is helpful if the company representative is someone who is respected by the employee rather than the person the employee sees as the bad actor.

Opposing attorneys might even consider talking with each other prior to the mediation about who should attend. A frank conversation between lawyers, mindful that participants who share mutual respect and trust increase the likelihood of a settlement, can be especially helpful.

4.

It's Never Too Late to Mediate

A couple of years ago, I received a call that went something like this:

> Michael, would you be willing to mediate a case this weekend? The trial starts next Tuesday. Yes, we want you to mediate three days before the trial starts. The money has been spent, and we're ready to go. It's probably a waste of time, but the judge wants us to try.

We mediated that case and settled it on a Saturday. If we had been unsuccessful, the lawyers were going to meet the next morning to try to agree on jury instructions.

There are many advantages of an early mediation. Precious resources haven't been spent. Stressful depositions haven't been taken. Lives and businesses haven't been interrupted. If I were involved in a difficult case, I would want to mediate it as early as I had enough information to make informed settlement decisions.

As a mediator, however, there are certainly advantages to a mediation in the late stages of a case. Lawyers frequently see eleventh hour mediations as long shots. These mediations, however, tend to have the greatest chance of success.

Kenneth Feinberg is, perhaps, the most successful mediator of our generation. His resume includes the September 11 Victim Compensation Fund, the BP oil spill, and the Penn State abuse scandal. His big break as a mediator came when he was appointed to mediate the Agent Orange class-action lawsuit in the 1980s. The plaintiffs had filed a 250,000-member class action on behalf of Vietnam veterans suffering the effects of the chemical known as Agent Orange. The trial was set for April 1984. The case had been pending for almost seven years. Feinberg was appointed to mediate the case only *eight weeks* before trial.

On the first day of mediation, the parties explained their settlement positions. The plaintiffs' first offer was $1.2 billion. The defendants said they would be willing to pay, collectively, $25,000. That's no typo. The plaintiffs' first offer was over a billion dollars. The defendants' first offer was in the low five figures.

Hopeless? Feinberg didn't think so. In fact, he saw the procedural posture—while painful for the parties—

as helpful to him. Years later, he explained, "When you go to mediate a case so close to trial like that, you're 75 percent home before you start."[1] He went on to say, "I don't care how complex it is. A trial date that is looming right around the corner is a big advantage to a mediator."[2]

On the day trial was scheduled to start, the case settled for $180 million, which was a record settlement at the time.

The moral of the story is not to wait until right before trial to mediate. In fact, the parties to that case likely wish they had mediated the case much earlier. A great deal of money, time, and stress was exhausted that could never be recovered. If you do find yourself on the eve of trial, however, don't think it's too late to give mediation a shot.

5.

What Should I Include in My Pre-mediation Statement?

Pre-mediation statements reveal a lot. They educate mediators on the facts, the law, and the procedural posture of the case. They also tell mediators something about the lawyer. Is the lawyer thorough? Is the lawyer willing to acknowledge weaknesses?

But what should be in a pre-mediation statement? I am asked this question constantly, especially by young lawyers. Two researchers have tried to answer this question with data.

Brian Farkas and Donna Erez-Navot teach alternative dispute resolution at Cardozo School of Law in New York. They conducted a survey of mediators, primarily in the commercial and employment fields, to determine their preferences regarding pre-mediation statements. Here are some of their findings:

Are Pre-Mediation Statements Requested?

- 66.67 percent: The percentage of respondents who "always" require pre-mediation statements.

- 14.44 percent: The percentage of respondents who "usually" require pre-mediation statements.

- 3.33 percent: The percentage of respondents who "rarely" or "never" require pre-mediation statements.[1]

Format and Tone

- 62.22 percent: The percentage of respondents who prefer pre-mediation statements in a single-spaced letter format.

- 5.56 percent: The percentage of respondents who prefer pre-mediation statements in a double-spaced format similar to a legal brief.

- 32.22 percent of respondents had specific preferences on the format of pre-mediation statements that were neither letter format nor a format similar to a legal brief. However, the authors noted that these special formats "seem to be formatted more as letters with topic headers than briefs."

- 94.44 percent: The percentage of respondents who wanted pre-mediation statements that are either "slightly" or "significantly" less formal than legal briefs.[2]

Length

- 46.67 percent: The percentage of respondents who prefer pre-mediation statements be less than ten single-spaced pages.

- 33.33 percent: The percentage of respondents who prefer pre-mediation statements be no more than five single-spaced pages.

- 4.44 percent: The percentage of respondents who would allow the limit to go to fifteen pages.[3]

Exhibits

- 82.22 percent: The percentage of respondents who "always" or "usually" want "relevant exhibits" attached to the pre-mediation statement.

- 42.22 percent: The percentage of respondents who want copies of the pleadings attached to the pre-mediation statement.[4]

Settlement Position

- 63.33 percent: The percentage of respondents "who ask advocates to include a specific statement regarding their clients' settlement position" in the pre-mediation statements.

- 20 percent: The percentage of respondents who like to see the party's "settlement range" in the pre-mediation statement.

- 7.78 percent: The percentage of respondents who do not want a party to disclose its settlement position or proposed settlement range.[5]

Legal Citations

- 58.89 percent: The percentage of respondents who want to see legal citations that have "a dispositive effect" on the claim.

- 31.11 percent: The percentage of respondents who want the pre-mediation statement to include "all relevant legal authority that could affect the outcome of the dispute."

- 10 percent: The percentage of respondents who generally do not want to see any legal citations in the pre-mediation statement or who only want them on a case-by-case basis.[6]

There are certainly trends in this survey. As this shows, however, specific mediators' preferences can vary widely. Pay attention to what your mediator asks for. If you're not sure, ask.

6.

Pre-mediation Telephone Calls with the Mediator Are Almost Always a Good Idea

I always encourage parties to have ex parte pre-mediation telephone calls with me. Some mediators require them as part of their engagement. I have never done this, as I don't want to appear to "work the file" just to bill more time. But I have always found calls with the lawyers in advance of the mediation helpful.

To be clear, I am not speaking of calls where both parties are on the telephone. Rather, I am referring to calls between the mediator and the advocate, without the other party's representative being on the phone. I have always found that lawyers are able to share useful nuggets "lawyer to lawyer" that perhaps they are hesitant to put down on paper when drafting the mediation statement. These might be items that are also in the mediation statement, but the advocate can stress to the mediator which considerations are especially important. The party might cite five cases in the mediation statement, but the inflection in a lawyer's voice might place special emphasis on a specific case.

In addition, there might be something driving a mediation that the lawyer feels more comfortable sharing verbally. I once mediated a case where the defendant had what I considered a defensible claim. I saw no reason why this defendant would want to settle at the mediation without first exporting some defenses through discovery. In a private telephone conversation, however, the company lawyer shared that the company was being sold in the near future and there was a fear on the part of the owner that the lawsuit might stall the sale. As it turns out, this was the issue that drove the mediation.

There may also be something about a client's personality or the personality of the opposing party (or opposing counsel) that a lawyer believes the mediator should know. Often these are things that the advocate does not feel comfortable putting in a mediation statement, even if they know it will be in confidence. There's just something more comfortable about sharing sensitive information verbally. It's human nature.

7.

Make Sure the Mediator Knows the Audience

It's surprising how often I find that I'm dealing with a decision maker different than who I thought. It is always best if the person with the checkbook attends the mediation. The process works the way it was intended to work when the decision maker is a full participant in the mediation process.

Even in cases where the ultimate decision maker is not in attendance, let your mediator know about the decision-making process. A good mediator will tailor their message to the audience. The message might be different if the decision maker is in-house counsel, an operations person, or an insurance carrier. In order to maximize the effectiveness of the mediator, ensure they know the audience.

8.

Tell the Mediator
What You Need

I was recently having lunch with a very good litigator. He was preparing for trial in the next couple of weeks. I asked him whether they had attempted mediation. He said something along the lines of, "Yes. It should have settled. My client has more exposure than they realize, but the mediator did not lean on my client as much as he should have."

My colleague was shocked by my follow-up question. "Did you tell the mediator that?" I asked. He said, "Of course not," adding that he did not tell the mediator to lean on his client. He explained he didn't think it was his job to convince the mediator to hammer on his own client. He thought he should convince the mediator to hammer on the other side.

The thing that my colleague missed is that the mediator is always looking for clues as to what the lawyer needs from him. A good mediator can be a chameleon. They can morph into various mediation styles. Do you need a facilitator? Do you need an arm twister? Do you need someone who can "reality check" with your client?

If a mediator is in a caucus room and the lawyer is aggressively debating each point that the mediator tries to make, the mediator might take this to mean that they are pushing too hard on the client.

By contrast, good lawyers frequently call me in advance of the mediation (or pull me aside before the mediation begins) to say, "This is a new client for me. I don't know them very well. But to give you a heads up, I think they are a bit too bullish on their case." This is the clue that the mediator needs to conclude that this party might need a more aggressive (but still diplomatic) evaluative mediator rather than a facilitative mediator, as we will discuss later.

9.

Pre-mediation Statements: To Share or Not to Share

When I litigated cases, I never shared my pre-mediation statement with my opposing counsel. I think there are some good reasons for this. If my pre-mediation statement was confidential, I could be very candid with the mediator about my strengths without causing acrimony with the other side. After all, I hired the mediator so they could have the hard conversations. I could also confidentially share my weaknesses, which both assisted the mediator and bolstered my credibility.

As a mediator, I still think this is often the best course. I want lawyers to be as candid with me as possible about both their strengths and their weaknesses. This is obviously easier to do if the pre-mediation statement is "for the mediator's eyes only."

Recently, however, I have experienced mediations where sharing the pre-mediation statement with the opposing party has been very effective. In light of this, consider two instances where you might consider sharing your pre-mediation statement with your opposing counsel.

First, consider a case where you know that your opposing party evaluates the case very differently than you do. Sharing your mediation statement with your opposing counsel in advance of the mediation will give them the opportunity to understand your evaluation and, perhaps, begin to think differently about this strength of their case. It will also give your opposing counsel the chance to discuss your evaluation of the case with their client and not just their own. I have found this is especially helpful when you have an opposing counsel with a very sophisticated client.

Second, sharing the pre-mediation statement with your opponent can be very useful when the case involves difficult legal nuances or complex damage calculations. I have found that good class-action lawyers on both sides are increasingly more likely to share their pre-mediation statements with each other in advance of the mediation session. These cases often involve the analysis of significant amounts of data in order to construct a damages model. While the parties may not agree how to view the data, it seems lawyers are deciding that it saves significant time at the beginning of mediation to share their data analysis (i.e., their damages model) prior to the day of the mediation.

10.

Alternatives to Mediation and Arbitration

The two types of ADR that receive the most attention are mediation and arbitration. Sometimes, however, it pays to be creative. Alternative dispute resolution is limited only by parties' creativity. Below are a few alternative forms of ADR.

Bracketed Arbitration: Bracketed arbitration is where the parties retain an arbitrator, but they place upper and lower limits on the arbitrator's discretion. For example, the parties may have agreed that $50,000 to $150,000 is an acceptable range for resolution, but they cannot agree on a number. In a bracketed arbitration, the parties would submit the dispute to an arbitrator, who would decide on a result in that range. The arbitrator is free to choose any number within this range. This protects the claimant from walking away with nothing while also protecting the respondent from an excessive decision.

Final Offer Arbitration: Sometimes called "baseball arbitration" because it is used by Major League Baseball and the Players' Association, this is where each party submits "final offers." If neither is accepted, the dispute is submitted to an arbitrator. The arbitrator's discretion is limited to choosing which of the final offers to adopt as the final award. This has the advantage of encouraging each party to make reasonable, good-faith offers, as the arbitrator's role is to adopt the most reasonable proposal.

Med/Arb: In a "Med/Arb" process, the parties submit the case to a traditional mediation. If the parties reach an impasse, the mediator's role changes. They become an arbitrator. This has advantage of bringing certain closure. The parties know going into the ADR process that they will emerge with a resolution: either a mediated settlement or an arbitrator's award. The disadvantage, of course, is that the parties may be less candid with the neutral if they believe the mediator may ultimately make the final decision.

Final Offer Med/Arb: This is a hybrid of the Med/Arb model and baseball arbitration. In this model, the neutral serves as a mediator in an effort to bring the parties to a mediated settlement. If the parties reach an impasse, the neutral becomes an arbitrator and makes an award. The neutral's discretion, however, is limited. They may only select which party's final offer to adopt.

11.

Self-Serving Bias

As I write this, the 2019 college football season is only one game old, but it has already gone south for me. As a proud graduate of the University of Tennessee, I believed we would return to respectability this year and finally field a good team. My hopes were dashed after the first game.

For the uninitiated, my alma mater has a tradition called the "Vol Navy." Fans ride their boats to the game, tie them to each other at the dock, and walk to the game together after a giant tailgate party on the water. Before the first game of the year even started, a boat in the Vol Navy caught fire and sank.

Things got worse from there. The weather was so hot during the first game that a member of the marching band passed out at halftime. Then there was the game itself. My beloved Volunteers, who I thought would finally have a good season, lost to a school that started their football program less than ten years ago. In case you're wondering, the University of Tennessee has been playing football since 1891.

It's clear my team is terrible again this year. How could I have been so wrong?

I had fallen victim to "self-serving bias," one of the most significant obstacles that mediators face during negotiations. Self-serving bias is a psychological process that causes us to perceive ourselves in an overly favorable manner. It prevents us from being objective about the things we love, own, or are attached to.

Those who have conducted significant research in the field of negotiations have observed that when parties enter into negotiations, they rarely have an accurate view of their likelihood of success if the negotiation is unsuccessful. They are influenced by self-serving bias. Accordingly, both parties look at their cases with rose-colored glasses, which distorts what their negotiating positions should be.

Plaintiffs, researchers tell us, have a more optimistic view of their claims than they should. Defendants, likewise, have a more optimistic view of their defenses than is objectively reasonable. This leads to statements like "The jury is going to give the plaintiff a blank check" or "The defendant is almost certain to get summary judgment." It's just like the start of football season. I had an overly optimistic view of my own football team. It's self-serving bias.

I think this is where good lawyers can truly help their clients. To combat self-serving bias, I think attorneys can do a few things:

- Lawyers should be aware of this phenomenon and caution their clients against it. "Claims [and defenses] are never as good as they seem" is usually good advice.

- Lawyers should be careful not to fall into this trap themselves. If an attorney takes on a client's cause to the point of losing their objectivity, they can lose their effectiveness. We've all seen this happen. Clients need objective advice. When a lawyer become too invested in their client's case, they fall victim to self-serving bias. In my view, this does the client a great disservice.

- If you see that your client is struggling with self-serving bias and is overly optimistic about the prospects of litigation, make sure your mediator knows this. The mediator can partner with you in addressing this during the mediation process. A good mediator knows about this issue and has developed strategies to help overcome it.

12.

Reactive Devaluation

"You know, the other side's offer is actually pretty fair."

These are words I never hear, and it's due to "reactive devaluation." This one of the most significant impediments to negotiated settlements I see.

Reactive devaluation is a cognitive bias that occurs when we devalue a proposal made by someone we oppose. Psychologists and researchers have conducted numerous studies that have confirmed the extent to which it can impact negotiations. For example, in a 2002 study published in the *Journal of Conflict Resolution*, the authors used an Israeli/Palestinian peace plan as the basis of their study. The researchers were four professors, two from the US and two from Israel. The participants were Israeli.

One group of the participants was told the peace plan was proposed by Israel. The other group was told that the source was Palestinian. The former rated the plan significantly higher than the latter. This, according to the authors, validated the role reactive devaluation played in finding a resolution to such ongoing hostilities.[1]

We see this in mediations every day. A plaintiff refuses to accept the defendant's "last offer," regardless of what it is. A defendant dismisses the plaintiff's bottom line, even if it is consistent with their own lawyer's evaluation. This is reactive devaluation at work, and we need to recognize it when it happens.

I think this is where a mediator and lawyer can be very helpful. It is important to counsel our clients to view proposals objectively, and it is important for lawyers not to fall victim to reactive devaluation. When we are at our best, attorneys can add a dispassionate evaluation to the other side's proposal. The most effective negotiators I work with are those who grab a good deal when it's on the table, regardless of who proposes it.

13.

Endowment Effect

Years ago, my wife inherited some land in rural Louisiana. Folks have offered to buy it from her, but she has never been interested. It's family land. We'll probably never live there. Heck, we only see it a few times per year. Nevertheless, it has been in my wife's family for ages. It would cost someone a fortune to even tempt her to sell it. Why? It's because of "endowment effect."

Behavioral economists tell us that the endowment effect is where we overvalue something that we own relative to how the market values it. In other words, we place a higher value on our own possessions than the market does.

We see this in negotiations every day. In commercial litigation, the founder of the company may place a greater value on the company than potential buyers. In IP litigation, the inventor will place greater value on her own intellectual property than investors would. Even in employment and civil rights litigation, we see parties take "ownership" of their claims, making them reluctant to settle their lawsuits for purely psychological reasons.

Endowment effect can be good or bad for your client, depending on how badly they need to reach a resolution.

If you don't necessarily need to reach a deal, endowment effect can be leveraged for greater concessions from your opposing party. You're holding a lot of the cards in a negotiation when you truthfully say, "I love my company . . . I built it from the ground up. I would consider selling it to you, but you're going to have to pay top dollar to tempt me."

By contrast, endowment effect can also lead your client to walk away from a really good deal. This is a big problem if your client needs to reach a resolution more than they appreciate.

In the course of an intense negotiation, it's important to recognize endowment effect when it happens. Sometimes you'll need to caution your client against endowment effect. Sometimes you can use it to your advantage in settlement talks. Sometimes it's just helpful to warn your client what they're dealing with when endowment effect takes hold of the other party. Regardless, a skilled negotiator will recognize and understand it.

Oh, and if you want to buy some of my wife's property in the backwoods of Louisiana, you better get your checkbook out. It's worth a fortune to her.

14.

Joint Sessions at the Beginning of a Mediation

In October 2018, I spoke at the ABA Advanced Mediation and Negotiation Institute in Chicago. I sat on a panel with a California mediator, an Atlanta attorney, and a Chicago attorney. The room was full of experienced mediators. The topic of our panel was "The Joint Session." Various perspectives emerged:

- "A joint session is just a waste of time."

- "I won't mediate without a joint session. I have to size up the other side."

- "I won't mediate if I have to see the other side."

- "It is important for the parties to talk to each other."

- "It will be a disaster if the parties talk to each other."

It seems everyone has an opinion. I wanted to share my thoughts on this topic, acknowledging that many excellent mediators disagree with me.

My default is for the parties to meet in a joint session at the beginning of the mediation, but I ask that counsel do not make opening statements. I am generally the only one who talks. Why do I do this?

First, it simply allows me to explain the process and ground rules of the mediation once rather than multiple times, depending on the number of parties.

Second, it allows me to set the tone of the discussion. By the nature of litigation, there's a dispute. People come into the mediation with hard feelings. I like to be first voice everyone hears, and I like to set a consolatory tone with everyone in the room. I think this is helpful.

Third, I believe a joint session helps decision makers who have never met the other party. Often, this is an insurance claims adjuster who only knows the plaintiff as a name in a file. At the conference in Chicago, for example, a claims adjuster from Birmingham commented that she would never participate in a mediation without having the opportunity to observe a plaintiff in a joint session.

I also understand there are many reasons not to have a joint session. I usually dispense with a joint session where are there are instances of alleged sexual misconduct, especially if the person accused is attending the mediation. If there is an unusually high level of acrimony between the parties, I also lean toward skipping the joint session. I also believe that self-determination is at the heart of mediation. If the parties do not want to have a joint session, then I honor that. I'm not the judge.

What's the takeaway? I encourage you to consider whether a joint session would be helpful or harmful in advance of the mediation. Talk to your client about it. Finally, communicate your thoughts to the mediator. A good mediator is flexible and understands the needs of every mediation is different.

15.

The First Private Caucus with the Mediator

I think we underestimate how important the first private meeting with the mediator can be. The mediator is your voice in the opposing party's room. For that reason, I think it is critical to be prepared for your first private caucus with the mediator. I encourage lawyers to have three or four points that they want to make to the mediator at the beginning of the mediation session. You are not trying to convince the mediator. They are not the judge. Rather, you want the mediator to know what is important to you. Otherwise, they cannot impress that upon your opposing party. In my view, you want to accomplish these things during your first private caucus:

1. Arm the mediator with your three or four strongest points.

2. Demonstrate to the mediator that you have a command of the facts and law.

3. Share a few (but not all) of your most compelling documents with the mediator.

4. If you have a significant weakness, go ahead and get it out on the table. You'll earn credibility, and the mediator is going to hear about it from the other side anyway.

16.

Some of the Most Important Work in a Mediation Is Done while the Mediator Is Outside the Room

I always tell parties to bring newspapers, magazines, or other reading material. I do this to acknowledge that a big part of mediation is waiting. When the mediator is outside your room and visiting with the other side in a private caucus, there is inevitably some downtime. However, I always encourage parties to take advantage of this downtime.

Some of the most important work in mediation is done while the mediator is outside the room and the lawyer is meeting privately with their client. The mediator will take time in private caucus to relay legal and factual arguments to your client. The mediator will also do a reality check. In other words, he will point out some weaknesses that perhaps the parties had not perceived.

Frequently, the advocate will push back against this reality checking. This is a good thing. It is important for the lawyer to arm the mediator with counterarguments that the mediator can take into the other room. However, once the mediator leaves your room, this is a valuable opportunity to talk candidly to the client about what they have just heard. A skilled mediator can tell whether, while they are outside the room, a lawyer has been helping their client process what they have just heard.

On more than one occasion, I have had a lawyer pull me aside and say, "I know that I gave you a lot of push-back when you were sharing the other side's arguments, but I want you to know that we are processing those while you are in the other room and your comments are helpful. They are having a good impact on my client." This tells me that I am working with a lawyer who is giving candid advice to their client and is using every minute of the mediation to their advantage, even when I am outside the room.

17.

Most Offers are a Response to the Last Offer

What to do if one party is unreasonably high or unreasonably low? Sometimes astute negotiators will be counterintuitive. Making a larger than expected move can prompt the other party to get reasonable. It shows a willingness to negotiate in good faith. It can also earn some credibility when you have to slow down with your moves later in the negotiation.

In the world of dispute resolution, this is called the "reciprocity norm." Professor Russell Korobkin explains:

> When people imagine a negotiation, they often conjure up visions of offers and counteroffers flying back and forth like a ping-pong ball across a table: the buyer makes a low offer, the seller responds with a high demand; the buyer raises

the offer, the seller in turn lowers his demand, and so forth until the positions of the parties converge. . . .

Social convention demands reciprocity. When one person gives something of value to another, we usually expect that the recipient will reciprocate in some way.[1]

Korobkin argues that this is at the heart of "the dance" we do in negotiation.[2]

What's the lesson? Take a chance. See what your opposing party does if you make a larger than expected concession. They might reciprocate.

18.

Judge Rosen's "Four Cs" of a Successful Mediation

I recently attended a presentation by former United States District Judge Gerald E. Rosen. Judge Rosen served as the chief mediator in the City of Detroit's bankruptcy case, one of the most consequential mediations of our time.

The Detroit bankruptcy case is a striking example of the power of mediation. It allowed the parties to reach a resolution—which they called the "Grand Bargain"— that could never have been reached through the courts. While there was a myriad of issues in the Detroit case, much of the dispute came down to two.

One the one hand, the city simply did not have the means to meet its pension obligations. Detroit is a fascinating example of a wealthy city that evolved into a struggling community. As an industrial economy gave way to a service and technology-based economy, Detroit lost both wealth and population. It simply could not meet its pension obligations. The city was in debt to the tune of $19 billion and had to file bankruptcy.

One the other hand, the City of Detroit owns one of the world's most impressive art collections. Detroit was once the fourth-largest city in the country. It was the center of wealth during the Industrial Revolution. This concentration of wealth during the early twentieth century is largely responsible for the Detroit Institute of Arts, widely regarded as the sixth-most valuable art collection in the world. Its holdings could be worth as much as $20 billion, and it was the city's only significant asset when it went into bankruptcy.

Detroit's pension debt and its vast art holdings resulted in both a legal and political showdown. Retirees relied on their pension. The professional class felt that losing the city's art museum would be akin to losing the soul of the city. This pitted the working class against the city's cultural elite.

Judge Rosen and a team of mediators spent thousands of hours working with the city, the state, creditors, unions, and various other stakeholders. The mediation resulted in the so-called "Grand Bargain." Reflecting on the experience, Judge Rosen speaks of the "Four Cs" necessary for a successful mediation: candor, cooperation, creativity, and courage.[1]

Candor: A case will not settle if a party is in denial about their weaknesses. Mediation is the confidential process where everyone can be honest about both their strengths and weaknesses. If a party cannot be candid with both the mediator and themselves about their weaknesses, the mediation is infinitely more difficult.

Cooperation: Litigation is an adversarial process. There's nothing wrong with that. For mediation to be successful, however, there must be a measure of cooperation. This usually means sharing documents and information. For a party to make an informed decision based on their risk, the opposing party has to be transparent about their evidence. This doesn't mean there are no secrets. Sometimes parties should hold onto information for strategic purposes. For mediation to be successful, however, parties often have to disclose more than they would like.

Creativity: The beauty of mediation is that you can do things in a negotiated settlement that a jury cannot do on a verdict form. According to Judge Rosen, "You must look for ways within the law but outside the box to find resolution."[2]

Courage: "If we're going to settle the case, they have to make a big move." Have you ever heard that? I hear it in almost every mediation. Rosen has apparently noticed the same thing. He commented, "Someone must be willing to overcome anger and rigidity and make a move they don't want to make."[3]

19.

Lessons from the Middle East

"When I was a young lawyer, we didn't have mediation." Have you heard respected lions of the trial bar say something like this? In reality, mediation has been around for ages. The United States legal system was just a bit slow to catch on.

In the Middle East, tribal leaders—called *shaykhs*— have served as mediators of disputes since antiquity. According to Middle Eastern tribal custom, when someone has wronged another, the victim's tribe has the right to exact vengeance on the perpetrator. To avoid this, the wrongdoer approaches their tribal leader to act as a mediator in the dispute. The shaykh assists the parties in negotiating a settlement. If the negotiation is successful, the alleged wrongdoer pays a financial settlement, and dispute is resolved. Sound familiar? In the

United States, we call this a mediated settlement. In the Middle East, it's called a *fasel*.

This process is well known to the US government. When the US military has injured or killed innocent civilians in the Middle East, they have frequently approached the tribal shaykh to negotiate a fasel.

The similarities between American mediations and this Middle Eastern process are remarkable. They are different, however, in at least two ways.

First, at the conclusion of the fasel, the parties to the dispute share a cup of coffee and a meal together. In all of my years as a lawyer and mediator, I've never seen the parties reach a mediated settlement and go grab a latte together at the Starbucks around the corner. I'm not holding my breath that it will happen anytime soon.

The other difference is just as striking. The alleged perpetrator in the Middle East generally seeks forgiveness from the alleged victim. In the US, "forgiveness" is replaced by "no admission of liability." In our system, I think we underestimate how important some measure of acknowledgement is to the plaintiff.

This was brought home to me in a recent sexual harassment case. The mediation was stalled. The plaintiff didn't want to make another move. The defendant thought that it had exposure but believed that the plaintiff was overvaluing the case. I asked the defendant if anything at the company had changed since this lawsuit was filed.

I learned that the company had enacted a new sexual harassment training program. I gathered details about this program and secured permission to discuss it with the plaintiff. For the next forty-five minutes, I didn't talk to the plaintiff about offers, damages, or chances of success. Instead, I explained the details of the company's new sexual harassment policy. It wasn't an apology, but it was close. It was, perhaps, the validation the plaintiff needed to become more willing to resolve the case.

At the end of the mediation, we signed a settlement agreement. The parties didn't break bread afterward, but perhaps we had more than a settlement. Perhaps we had a fasel.[1]

20.

Pragmatism over Principle

I frequently write about successful negotiations and the lessons that we can learn from them. Sometimes, however, failed negotiations teach us even greater lessons.

A legend among Tennessee lawyers, Lewis R. Donelson III passed away on January 4, 2018, at the ripe old age of 100. Known as "Lewie," Donelson is credited with building the Tennessee Republican Party, growing a major law firm, and contributing to the fall of a corrupt governor who went to prison for selling liquor licenses. A political moderate, Lewie often spoke about the importance of compromise and finding a way to settle disputes. His life experiences taught him these lessons.

In 1968, Lewie Donelson served on the Memphis City Council. Faced with low wages and unsafe working conditions, Memphis sanitation workers went out on strike in February of that year. They held signs that read, "I AM A MAN." Martin Luther King Jr. came to Memphis in March of 1968 to support the striking workers, but his appearance was cut short due to an outbreak of violence. Determined to hold a nonviolent demonstration, Dr. King planned a return visit in April.

Meanwhile, Lewie Donelson worked tirelessly to persuade the city to settle the strike. The mayor and other city council members refused. They argued that it would be inappropriate to negotiate with the workers' union because state law did not recognize its existence. Moreover, there was no money in the budget to give them the pay raise they were seeking. Lewie secured the funds for a raise from a private benefactor and developed a legal framework that would have allowed the city to settle the dispute without recognizing the union. Still, the mayor and city council chose to stand on principle.

In an effort to ease tensions, Lewie proposed resolutions proclaiming the city an equal opportunity employer and setting up a civil rights commission. Mayor Henry Loeb said, "Look here, Lewie, on my desk there's 130 letters about your two resolutions, 128 of them against, and 2 of them for. What do you think of that?" Lewie just said, "I didn't think we were elected to count letters."[1]

As it turned out, the city didn't give in to Lewie's efforts to negotiate a settlement with the sanitation workers. The strike continued. Dr. King returned to

Memphis and was gunned down on April 4, 1968. The history of Memphis and the nation were permanently altered.

In his memoir, Lewie Donelson reflected on the consequences of the city's refusal to settle. He wrote, "In effect [after the King assassination], the strike was over. The mayor caved in under national and local pressure. . . . The impact of the strike on Memphis, however, was devastating; it took at least twenty years before the city recovered. Nashville moved ahead of Memphis, and Memphis lost its premier place in Tennessee and among the leading cities of the South."[2]

As lawyers, we frequently hear people say they will not settle based on principle. In my mediations, I tell parties that they can have all the principle they can afford. Principle, however, comes at great cost. It costs money, time, interrupted lives, interrupted businesses, and the stress of an uncertain outcome. The lessons of Memphis in 1968 also teach us that refusing to settle can come with unforeseen costs.

History will remember Lewie Donelson for his many accomplishments. I will remember him as someone who understood the importance of compromise and settlement.

As a happy postscript, Memphis is celebrating its bicentennial as I write this. I wish Mr. Donelson would have lived to see it. Recent years have seen much progress. There's so much to celebrate about Memphis. Its food. Its music. Its culture. Its people. My wife and I are proud graduates of the University of Memphis. She received her undergraduate degree from the U of M, and I attended their law school. We get back to the Bluff City as often as we can. Memphis has so much to offer, and its history has so much to teach us.

21.

Risk: It's More Important than Facts

Having a mediation practice is interesting for a variety of reasons. One reason is the eclectic cast of characters that roll through my office. Occasionally, someone will say something like this to me: "Michael, you don't have to tell me about the mediation process. I'm an experienced negotiator."

When I hear this, I stop everything and explain that negotiating the settlement to a lawsuit is unlike other types of negotiations. When you buy a piece of real estate, you negotiate based on facts. How old is the house? Does it have a new roof? Will the HVAC system need to be replaced soon?

When you buy a car, you negotiate based on facts. How many miles does it have on it? Has it been serviced regularly? Can I kick the tires?

When you buy a business, you negotiate based on facts. What do the financials look like? How about the balance sheet?

You get the picture.

Lawsuits are a different animal. Parties frequently say to me, "The story they're telling is not factually true. I'm not even going to consider it." This misses the whole point of a mediation. In a lawsuit, we don't negotiate based on facts. We negotiate based on risk. In my view, you do your clients a valuable service if you help them understand the concept of "litigation risk" when they prepare for the mediation. Explain that the questions we ask in a mediation look very different than the questions that are asked in other negotiations:

- Regardless of whether it's true, what is the risk the jury will believe my opponent?

- Regardless of whether it's fair, what is the risk the judge will agree with their view of the law?

- Regardless of whether it's honest, what is the risk the witness will support their side of the story?

- Regardless of whether it's right, what is the risk the jury won't believe you?

A good mediator will help your client understand this dynamic, but you can go a long way toward increasing the likelihood of a successful negotiation if you lay the groundwork prior to the mediation. When a party in one of my mediations says, "That's just not true," I usually respond by asking, "But is there a risk the jury might believe them?" In my view, this is what drives a mediation.

22.

It Pays to Be Nice

There are various mediation styles. A lot of time has been spent by academics trying to determine which type of personality yields the best negotiation results. While the hard-nosed, scorched-earth personality tends to get much attention, research almost uniformly concludes that negotiators who build trust and relationships with their opposing party reach the best results for their clients.

Research by Professor Janice Nadler at Northwestern University suggests that parties can get better results in their negotiations simply by chatting with their opponent for five minutes on the telephone—not by email—about matters other than the issues to be negotiated. In other words, Professor Nadler argues that the research proves that it pays to schmooze.[1]

Professor Charles B. Craver at George Washington University is one of the country's foremost experts in negotiation strategies. He has observed:

> When negotiators begin to interact, they should take the time to establish rapport with each other and positive bargaining settings. At the outset, they should look for common interests they can share with each other. They may have attended the same college or law school, enjoy the same sports or music, etc. Persons who can identify and share such common interests enhance the likelihood they will like each other and develop mutually beneficial relationships. Such circumstances contribute to the establishment of rapport and increase the likelihood the participants will employ cooperative behavior during their discussions.
>
> The initial portions of bargaining interactions are also critical, because it is when the parties create the atmosphere that will influence their entire encounter. If their discussions begin on an unpleasant or distrusting note, subsequent talks are likely to be less open and more adversarial than if the process had begun in a congenial and cooperative manner. Negotiators who induce their adversaries to like them, and who treat their opponents respectfully and professionally, are more likely to obtain beneficial results than bargainers who do not generate such sympathetic feelings.[2]

When parties and lawyers come to a mediation, one of the first things I observe is whether there is a measure of acrimony between any of participants. We are certainly able to settle cases where folks don't like each other. In fact, this is where a mediator can be especially helpful. However, I think lawyers often underestimate how valuable building trust with the opposing counsel can be. Research suggests that parties make quicker concessions to opponents they trust and with whom they have established a relationship.

23.

Focus on Interests

I write this on February 11, 2020, exactly thirty years after Nelson Mandela was released from prison. Like many of you, I recall the end of apartheid unfolding on the evening news. I have a clear memory of reading Mandela's book *Long Walk to Freedom* during my junior year at the University of Tennessee. Almost three decades later, that book still has a prominent place on my bookshelf. Without question, apartheid was one of the most significant atrocities of the twentieth century.

I recently watched the movie *Endgame*. No, not the superhero movie. The 2009 movie *Endgame* details the negotiations which led to Mandela's release and the end of apartheid. It's a great movie, and you should watch it. But I suppose I'm a bit biased. After all, how many movies are made about a mediator?

Endgame introduces viewers to Michael Young, the British businessman who mediated the negotiations between the African National Congress (the ANC) and surrogates to the South African government. One especially dramatic scene depicts an exchange between Professor Willem Esterhuyse, who represented the interests of the government, and Thabo Mbeki, who represented the ANC.

In this scene, Mbeki challenges Esterhuyse regarding his position on majority rule in South Africa. Professor Esterhuyse lets down his guard. Instead of restating his position, he shared his interests. He said, "Our fear stems from our knowledge that one day we will be punished for the terrible wrongs we have inflicted."[1] According to this telling of the story, the South African government was interested in maintaining control of the institutions of government primarily because they feared retaliation by the ANC.

What followed the end of apartheid was remarkable. The South Africa Truth and Reconciliation Commission was one of the most successful dispute resolution programs ever created. It was constituted to bring closure, reward transparency, promote reconciliation, and avoid retaliation. In other words, it addressed the interests of both sides of the conflict. It happened because good negotiators made wise decisions. It also happened because the mediator, Michael Young, steered those negotiators toward focusing on interests rather than positions.

Three decades later, we can still learn from those difficult days. When negotiating, take the time to ask the other party, *"Why?* Why is a confidentiality clause important to you? Why is it important that you retain an ownership interest in the company? Why is it important that you be allowed to keep a copy of these records?" Move past the party's position and ask about their interests. This is especially important when negotiating noneconomic terms.

Good negotiators are constantly searching for ways to meet the other party's interests. They can only do this, however, if they know what those interests are.

24.

Mediation While a Dispositive Motion Is Pending

Much has been written about the "best" time to mediate. The short answer, in my view, is that there is *not* a best time. I think mediation should be considered as soon as the parties have enough information to make informed decisions.

I am never asked, however, about the "worst" time to go to mediation. My answer may surprise you. I often find that people go to mediation after summary judgment is briefed but before it is decided. I suppose litigants reason that this is the point where the parties have the most at risk, so they should be more motivated to find a resolution. Research, however, suggests the opposite.

Roselle L. Wissler is the research director at the Lodestar Dispute Resolution Program at the Arizona State University College of Law. In 2002, she published an article in the *Ohio State Journal on Dispute Resolution,* which examined the success of the ADR program in Ohio courts. According to Wissler's research, cases are actually least likely to settle at mediation while a dispositive motion is pending.[1]

My experience is consistent with Professor Wissler's findings. As I have written about previously, each side has a cognitive bias that leads them to an overly optimistic view of their case. When summary judgment is pending, it is usually at the point in the case where the parties' perspectives are most at odds. Therefore, it can be the most difficult time to try to settle.

To be sure, we have plenty of successful mediations while a motion for summary judgment is pending. I am certainly not discouraging the parties from mediating while a motion is pending. To maximize the chances of settlement, however, Wissler concluded that "[c]ases were more likely to be settled if mediation was held sooner after the case had been filed."[2]

25.

The First Offer Matters

As a mediator, my job would be much easier if the plaintiff would make a reasonably low opening offer. I would then like the defendant to respond with a reasonably high opening offer. That would put everyone in a good mood, and I could be on the tennis court by four thirty.

This, of course, is not the real world of negotiations. In the real world, both plaintiffs and defendants agonize over their opening offer. But do opening offers matter? The research suggests they do. In a 1999 article for *The Trial Lawyer* magazine, V. Hale Starr observes that the majority of plaintiff's lawyers expect to recover 20 to 50 percent of their opening offer. Similarly, a small offer by a defendant is rarely reflective of how he or she truly values the case.[1]

Opening offers are important because of "anchoring." Generally speaking, a high first offer from the plaintiff causes the defendant to think they may have to pay more to settle the case. A very low first offer from the defendant makes a plaintiff think they may have to take less to settle the case. If a party readjusts their expectations after receiving a first offer, they have been "anchored."

In 2006, Chris Guthrie, dean of the Vanderbilt Law School, published an article on this topic with Professor Dan Orr in the *Ohio State Journal of Dispute Resolution*. According to Guthrie and Orr's research, "An opening offer and initial counteroffer account for 57.6 percent of the variance in negotiated outcomes."[2]

This research comes with two big caveats. First, your first offer must be realistic. As Professors Deepak Mahortra and Max Bazerman of Harvard Business School have written, "You should never make an offer so extreme that it cannot be stated as follows: 'I would like to propose X, because . . . .'"[3] In other words, there must be rationale behind your first offer.

Second, if you're a plaintiff, you cannot stay too high for too long. And as a defendant, you cannot stay too low for too long. You must show movement with your counteroffers. Otherwise, settlement will become unattractive, and your opponent will lose interest in trying to reach a negotiated resolution. Once you have set your anchor, your "concession pattern" must show a willingness to compromise.

26.

Let Your Clients Talk

I often find that lawyers want to "protect" their client. "You don't have to talk if you don't want to" is something I often hear. This not only does a disservice to clients but also decreases the chances of a mediation being successful.

In *Designing Systems and Processes for Managing Disputes,* the authors observe, "Research suggests that individuals care a great deal about the dispute resolution process and not just the result they reach through it. . . . What tends to matter in terms of fairness perceptions is that the process affords them the *opportunity to be heard* [emphasis added], that the process be even-handed and respectful, and that the process be viewed as trustworthy."[1]

In my view, this is one of the most significant reasons that mediations are more effective in negotiating settlements than one-on-one negotiations. Asking a litigant to give up their opportunity to have their case heard is a more difficult ask than most lawyers appreciate. A fair and neutral mediation, where each side has the opportunity to be heard, often serves as the dispute resolution process the litigant craves.

Psychology professor Tom Tyler, who has studied what he calls "procedural justice," has concluded that four factors determine whether a party feels like a process conforms to their desire for procedural justice:

- "[P]eople want the opportunity to state their case to the authorities."

- "[P]eople expect neutrality of the authority's decision-making process."

- "[P]eople also value the quality of their interpersonal treatment by the authorities, that is, whether they feel they are being treated with dignity and respect by the legal authorities."

- "[P]eople focus on cues that communicate information about the intentions and character of the legal authorities with whom they are dealing."[2]

While I am certainly not the decision maker in a mediation, litigants often see me as something of an authority figure in the process. Because of this, I try very hard to create an atmosphere of procedural fairness in the mediation process that will increase the likelihood of its success.

The most important thing that a lawyer can do to help is simply let their clients talk if they want to.

27.

Bidding Against Yourself: The Rejection and Retreat Technique

When I was an undergraduate at the University of Tennessee, I had the perfect job for a future mediator. I asked people for money. Every Thursday night, I would walk across campus to the basement of the old basketball arena and sit down behind a computer screen. I, along with a room full of other students, would call alumni and ask for donations. Yes, I was a telemarketer.

I still remember the script: *My name is Michael Russell. I'm a sophomore at the University of Tennessee. Thank you for your contributions to UT over the years. Can the university count on you for a $500 donation tonight? No? Well, I certainly understand. Do you think you would be able to donate $100?"*

Here's the thing. We never expected to get the $500. If we did, great. But that wasn't the goal. The goal was to get the $100 donation. And we usually did.

When I began studying negotiation theory, I realized the brilliance of the approach. This is what negotiation scholars call the "rejection and retreat" technique. You make an offer you suspect will be rejected, and then you "bid against yourself" by making a more reasonable proposal. Multiple studies have demonstrated the effectiveness of this technique.

We've all been in negotiations where we were told, "That offer is ridiculous; I'm not responding to it." The temptation is to declare an impasse. The research, however, clearly shows that bidding against yourself usually produces a favorable response.

Try it. Then tell your client, "That's the old rejection and retreat technique . . . works every time."

28.

Put the Cart before the Horse: Should We Start with a Settlement Agreement?

When I was a litigator and preparing for trial, I would always write my closing argument first. One of my mentors told me, "You can't tell the jury where to go unless you know what the destination looks like." That was sage advice to a 26-year-old lawyer, and I followed it every case I took to trial. I think it works in negotiations too.

In most mediations, the parties will negotiate, haggle, threaten to leave, and then settle their case. After they agree on a number, they'll put pen to paper and draft a memorandum of understanding, which will memorialize the terms of the settlement. The lawyers will then go to their offices and begin work on a more formal agreement. Sometimes, we'll even try to hammer out the final agreement before we leave the mediation. Even then, the drafting usually doesn't start until the parties have reached an agreement in principle.

In complex litigation, however, astute lawyers will often make an opening offer in the form of a proposed memorandum of understanding. I've noticed this is especially helpful in complicated business disputes and class actions.

Instead of simply receiving a number, their opponent receives a detailed proposal which sets forth all aspects of a potential settlement. Of course, it's just a first offer. There's always significant room to negotiate. In a negotiation where there are many moving parts, however, sharing a proposed memorandum of understanding early in the negotiation guarantees that you're not talking apples while the other side is hearing oranges.

In an employment class action, for example, it's often a problem to wait until the parties arrive at "the number" to begin asking questions such as

- Who will pay for the class administrator?

- Will taxes be paid from outside the settlement fund?

- Will there be a *cy pres*?

- What happens if all of the settlement fund isn't claimed?

- How will class notice be sent?

• What will class notice say?

How the parties answer these questions may influence the final number, so it's often wise to start talking about them early. Sending a proposed memorandum of understanding with a party's opening offer can help identify problems at the outset of the case. If there's a major noneconomic term that could be an obstacle to settlement, everyone should know about it sooner rather than later.

To be clear, in cases where the only issue is money, the settlement documents usually fall into place fairly easily. However, if you have a complicated case with multiple material terms, consider sending a proposed memorandum of understanding to your opponent in advance of the mediation. You can't lead them to your destination unless they know what you want it to look like.

29.

Riskin's Grid: Do You Need a Facilitator or an Evaluator?

Leonard Riskin is a renowned law professor and ADR scholar who taught at the University of Missouri during the 1990s. During this time, Professor Riskin set out to observe mediations and write about the work of people who call themselves "mediators." The result is what has been called "Riskin's Grid" or "Riskin's Grid of Mediation Techniques."

According to Riskin, there are two continuums where mediators function. First, he wrote that mediators ranged from being "facilitative" mediators to being "evaluative" mediators.[1] Second, he said that mediators ranged from defining the problem "narrowly" to defining the problem "broadly."[2] He illustrated his observations on in a grid that, while it has evolved over time, generally looks like the diagram shown here.[3]

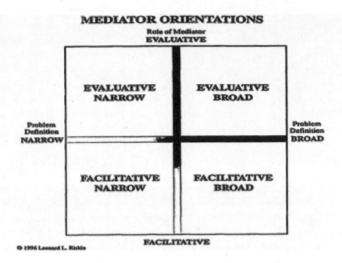

MEDIATOR ORIENTATIONS

Role of Mediator
EVALUATIVE

EVALUATIVE NARROW	EVALUATIVE BROAD
FACILITATIVE NARROW	FACILITATIVE BROAD

Problem Definition NARROW

Problem Definition BROAD

FACILITATIVE

© 1996 Leonard L. Riskin

As for the difference between a broadly defined problem and a narrowly defined problem, well, I'll write about that later. For now, I want to address an evaluative mediator versus a facilitative mediator.

At first blush, you might think of an evaluative mediator as a classic arm twister. By contrast, some would say that a facilitative mediator is a more passive neutral who keeps their opinions to themselves. This, however, is far too simplistic. I believe that a skilled mediator can (and should) function anywhere along Riskin's Grid. The key, in my view, is for a mediator to determine where he or she needs to function at any given time.

For example, an insurance adjuster who has been through a million mediations might want a mediator who will share their views very early in the process. In other words, this negotiator may want a mediator who functions strictly at the top of the grid.

A general counsel may be firm in their own evaluation of a case and may refuse to engage with a mediator who tries to share their views. This person will want a mediator at the bottom of the grid.

A victim of sexual assault may need to be heard and validated before they are willing to negotiate. This person may need a mediator who functions at the bottom of the grid early in the mediation and then becomes more evaluative once they have earned the party's trust.

The attitude of your client is important in each of these situations. During a mediation, the mediator will often explore how evaluative or facilitative they need to be. It's important for lawyers to remember that they know their client far better than the mediator does. One of the most important things you can do for your client in preparing for a mediation is to consider what mediation techniques will be helpful. Sharing those views with the mediator in advance of the mediation will go far in helping the mediator properly manage the negotiation. In other words, help the mediator understand where on Riskin's Grid they need to function.

30.

"Riskin's Grid": How Broad Is the Problem?

In the last chapter, I wrote about Professor Leonard Riskin's Grid of Mediator Orientations.

As a quick refresher, Leonard Riskin is one of the pioneers in ADR. When he was on the law faculty at the University of Missouri, he wrote a groundbreaking article about what people who call themselves mediators actually do. His "grid" is illustrated in the last chapter.[1] There, I discussed his observation that mediators ranged from being facilitative to evaluative.[2] Professor Riskin also observed that some mediators defined the problem being mediated narrowly, while some mediators defined the problem broadly.[3]

A narrowly focused mediator might be only interested in the facts, law, damages, and likelihood of trial success. By contrast, a mediator who viewed problems broadly might ask questions such as

- How much stress will this litigation cause you?

- Are you concerned about publicity?

- Are you risk averse?

- Is business interruption a concern?

- Might this litigation interfere with your relationship with other customers?

- Can the plaintiff afford to wait for trial?

- Can the defendant afford to fight through appeal?

In my view, a good mediator should be able to define a problem narrowly or broadly, depending on the needs of a case. Lawyers can help both their clients and the mediator by exploring this prior to the mediation. As a mediator, I often urge lawyers to help me understand their clients' interests. This will inform how broadly or narrowly I manage a mediation caucus.

For example, an insurance adjuster may only be interested in the facts, law, and risk. This person may benefit from a narrowly framed mediation. The CEO of a nonprofit may be concerned about the impact of publicity on donors. This person may benefit from a broadly framed mediation. A wealthy plaintiff in a breach of contract case may want a narrowly focused mediation, while a plaintiff who has suffered significant emotional trauma in a sexual assault case will need a mediation framed more broadly.

You are doing your client a great service if you explore the breadth of your client's interests prior to the mediation and help your mediator know how to frame the negotiation.

31.

Timing Is Everything

Negotiation is about communication, and it's not just verbal communication. We negotiate by what we say, but we also negotiate by how we say it. In a mediation, parties rely on the mediator for much of the verbal communication. This is productive. Part of the philosophy behind mediation is that your opponent will respond more favorably to your messages if they are delivered by a neutral party.

However, there other ways a party communicates to their opponent in a mediation. The most obvious nonverbal method of communication in a negotiation is simply the size of the offers. A $10 million opening demand from a plaintiff communicates something vastly different than a $100,000 opening demand.

Often overlooked, however, is what the *pace* of negotiation communicates. If you respond to an offer quickly, it often communicates decisiveness and, perhaps, that you're pleased with the offer you received from the other side. It might also communicate an over eagerness to settle. On the other hand, quick offers and counteroffers often build momentum, causing parties to negotiate cooperatively and efficiently.

If it takes you a while to respond to an offer in a mediation, that communicates something else. But what? It may communicate that you're struggling to respond to your opponent's last offer because you didn't see it as productive. Indeed, it may communicate a reluctance to respond at all. Slow offers may also communicate disagreement between the decision makers on your side. If it takes you some time to respond to an offer in a mediation, your opponent may believe that the decision makers in your room are having trouble "getting on the same page."

Negotiation is communication. Mediators can help with your messaging and delivery. We're trained to communicate information and proposals in a way that is constructive. The parties, however, can still communicate to their opponent in strategic ways. Sometimes, timing is everything.

32.

Don't Introduce Incendiary Settlement Terms

When I was a trial lawyer, I loved to tell stories of courtroom exploits. If I'm brutally honest, they may have grown more impressive the more I told them. I've also walked out of the courtroom on the wrong end of a decision. Here's the thing about being a trial lawyer: sometimes you're the hammer . . . sometimes you're the nail. Somehow, it's only the victories that find their way into the stories that lawyers tell.

Mediators are the same. We remember every failed mediation, but we don't like to talk about them. Now I want to tell you about one of my mediations that went astray a few years ago. It's a case that *didn't* settle.

I had a mediation where the parties were making significant progress. Near the end of the mediation, one of the parties wanted to propose a noneconomic term that I knew the other side would find offensive. To make it even more frustrating, I suspected they were only introducing this incendiary term to take a jab at the other party.

I asked them not to propose the term. I warned them it would be counterproductive. But they insisted. In fact, they gently reminded me that it was their mediation, and they could propose any term they darn well pleased.

As diplomatically as I could, I communicated the offer to the other side. They exploded. "I've never been so offended in my life," they said. As they packed their bags, they added, "We're leaving."

I then told the party who had made the offer that, as I predicted, their proposal may have ended the negotiations. They immediately realized they have overplayed their hand. They wanted a deal, they said. They tried to walk back the proposal.

It was too late. The incendiary term in the proposal had destroyed any chance of getting the case settled at mediation. Fortunately, everyone calmed down during the following days. I was able to facilitate a series of phone calls after the mediation, and the case eventually settled. But those efforts were completely unnecessary.

To be sure, negotiations involve difficult conversations. Proposing terms that you know will make the other side angry simply to score points, however, is not effective negotiation. As I often say, you serve your clients best when you save the theatrics for the jury.

33.

How Important Is the Mediation to Your Client?

If you have lived through a mediation with me, you know that I have some canned opening remarks I make at the beginning of the process. I talk about my role as a neutral. I talk about confidentiality. I talk about the importance of compromise. Like any lawyer worth their salt, I also talk about myself. A good friend recently asked, "How can you do that every day?" It would drive him crazy, he said.

I have given my initial mediator's monologue well over a thousand times. Do I get tired of it? Yes. Do the lawyers get a little tired of it too? Probably, if they were honest with me. Will I stop doing it? Absolutely not.

I've explained the process of mediation, its benefits, its confidentiality rules, and the importance of compromise so often, I could recite it in my sleep. Lawyers have heard it from me to the point they can recite it themselves. *The parties, however, may be hearing it for the first time.*

I teach an alternative dispute resolution course at the Belmont University College of Law in Nashville. During one class, I asked Greg Parent to be my guest speaker. Greg is a fantastic mediator in Atlanta. He is also a tremendously charismatic speaker. A significant part of Greg's practice is mediating catastrophic injury cases.

During his talk, Greg looked out over my class of third-year law students and said, "Don't ever let mediation become routine. In every mediation, that day may be one of the most important days in someone's life."[1]

That's true. As a lawyer, I often forgot that. As a mediator, I try to remember. That's why I say the same thing every day: I'm a neutral third party. This mediation is confidential. You can be candid with me because a judge and jury will never hear what we talk about. I want to hear what you have to say. If we have a settlement, it will require you to compromise. There is no shame in compromise. A mediated settlement is better than the alternative."

When I was an advocate, I complained about mediators who said the same thing over and over. The truth, however, is that I was often complacent. I sometimes didn't adequately prepare my client for the mediation. I sometimes assumed my client knew more about the process than they actually did. I didn't stop to consider how important this case was to my client. It may have involved their life, their job, their livelihood, their business, or their financial stability.

Mediation has become so routine for so many of us, we too often forget that it's not just another day for our clients. At the beginning of every mediation, let's stop and consider how important the day is to the people in each room.

34.

Brainstorm with Your Mediator

A skilled mediator will, without exception, talk his way into your brainstorming sessions with your client. He or she will want to be involved in the process. To be sure, the advocate's interest will not be completely aligned with the mediator's interest. The mediator wants to get a deal; you want to get the *best* deal.

However, you both want to get a deal done. The mediator is an important tool, as they have some knowledge that you do not: they know what is going on in the other room. The mediator is aware of the buttons they are pushing that might be helpful and is also aware of concerns that you might not know about.

Because of the confidentiality of the mediation process, the mediator cannot share these things with you. The mediator, however, can brainstorm with you. I have often had people say, "We are thinking about making this offer. How do you think they will respond to it?" This is music to a mediator's ears. This allows them to get integrally involved in the negotiating process. Without betraying any confidence, the mediator can help you identify the things you don't mind putting on the table and that the other side wants. In my view, this can be a win-win for both parties.

I have also had litigants ask, "Are there any non-economic terms that you think might entice them?" Obviously, the mediator may have been told something in confidence that they cannot share. There may be something, however, that they have been given free rein to share and have been holding in their hip pocket until this exact time. Invite the mediator to share this. Even if the mediator knows something that is confidential, perhaps the mediator can use this as an opportunity to persuade the other party to let them reveal it.

The mediator can be a valuable resource in formulating your offers. Obviously, the mediator is not representing your client. The mediator's job is not to get your client the best deal they can. Moreover, you probably know things the mediator does not know. However, allowing the mediator to be a sounding board in formulating your offers and counteroffers can be very productive. Perhaps it is at the core of their usefulness.

35.

The "Bottom Line" Is Likely to Change

After two hours into a mediation, I often hear parties complain that their time is being wasted at mediation. They say things like "They are not negotiating in good faith" or "We'll never get their number" or "They will never get to *our* number."

I have no doubt that these are sincere expressions of frustration. People believe it when they say it. These comments, however, overlook an important part of the negotiation process. When litigants come to a mediation, they often have "their number." For plaintiffs, this is the least they are willing to take. For defendants, this is the most they are willing to pay. Those who study and teach dispute resolution call this a party's "reservation point." If there's an overlap, then the mediation will go smoothly. If there's not an overlap, however, one or both parties will have to change their reservation point to get a deal. This, in my view, is the great strength of mediation.

Most of the time, people learn things in a mediation. They see new weaknesses in their case. They view risk in a new light. They learn things about their own tolerance for litigation. Minds change. People become invested in the process. Mediation gives both sides an opportunity to reassess with the help of a neutral and in the context of a confidential proceeding.

Simply put, people do things at the end of a mediation that they were not willing to do at the beginning of a mediation. In most successful mediations, both sides end up agreeing to things that they would never have agreed to hours earlier. Do not be discouraged by frustrations early in the day.

36.

Don't Back Your Opponent into a Corner

Thirteen Days: A Memoir of the Cuban Missile Crisis by Robert F. Kennedy is a great history book. It's also a great mediation book. You know the story. Many of you lived through it. Here's the (extremely) short version: The Cuban government was in the process of installing Soviet nuclear missiles in Cuba, ninety miles off the coast of the United States. The United States insisted they be moved. The Soviets refused. The two countries were at cusp of an impasse, like many mediations.

Unlike many mediations, however, this particular impasse could have brought the world to an end.

The United States had backed the Soviets into a corner. They had blockaded ships coming into Cuba, and many advisors were urging President John F. Kennedy to invade. Instead of taking the most aggressive approach, however, President Kennedy decided to give the Soviets a way out.

The United States had missiles too. They were in Turkey, and the Soviets didn't like them there. Truthfully, they were outdated. Some questioned whether they were even operable. Some sources suggest that the US was planning to remove them later in the year.

Nevertheless, the United States and the Soviets worked out a trade. The Soviets would first remove the missiles from Cuba, and the US would then remove their missiles from Turkey. Kennedy allowed the Soviets a graceful way to remove the Cuban missiles, avoid a nuclear conflict, and do it while claiming to have won a concession from the United States. In other words, the Soviets were backed into a corner, and the US allowed them to leave with their pride intact.

This is how skilled negotiators manage mediations when they have all of the leverage. Instead of saying things like "take it or leave it," they look for ways to help the opposing party feel they have gotten something.

Try it. The next time you're in a negotiation and clearly have the upper hand, remember that there is likely a prideful party in the other room, accompanied by a lawyer who trying to get the best deal they can for their client. Instead of trying to bend their will, look for concessions that you really don't mind making anyway.

Why should you do this? Well, for one thing, it will make the negotiation go smoother and more efficiently for your client. Second, the next time you have a case with the same lawyer, the shoe might be on the other foot.

37.

It's Healthy to Let Go

It's hard to let go. In Nashville, people hang on to lost loves until they turn into a country music song. In lawsuits, people hang on to their litigation. Some people don't want closure; they want to fight. When a fair compromise is on the table, sometimes they just want to hang on and fight a little longer. This can be a significant obstacle to settlement.

It's also unhealthy.

The Program on Negotiation at Harvard Law School recently published an interesting blog post on this topic. The author observed that parties "often fail to recognize when it's time to walk away from a negotiation dispute—a trap that can squander time, money, and reputations."[1] She points to Tyler and Cameron Winklevoss as prime examples.[2] They were twins who sued Facebook for allegedly stealing their concept. The brothers reached a settlement with Facebook for $65 million. That's life-changing money! Objective observers viewed it as huge win.

The problem? They were too emotionally invested. They tried to back out of the settlement. They eventually sued their lawyers and asked an appellate court to set aside the deal. After losing at every turn, they eventually gave up the fight.

I have seen this play out too many times. Parties become so emotionally attached to their lawsuit, they fail to see what is, in actuality, a fair deal. It happens to plaintiffs, business owners, and even to lawyers. People become emotionally attached to their cause. They fail to see how unhealthy their attachment is. It causes them stress, anxiety, and unrealistic expectations of what a judge or jury will do.

This is where good lawyers and mediators are important. Lawyers are attorneys and *counselors* at law. As the author at Harvard observes, "In negotiation, as in other spheres of life, it can be difficult to recognize when the pursuit of a goal becomes a destructive obsession. Here again, discussions with a trusted counselor can help you recognize when it's time to let go."[3]

What can be done? First, prepare your client for negotiations. It's their case. They have a right to their day in court. However, lawyers should encourage clients to compromise if it is in their best interest. Second, explain the benefits (both financial and psychological) of closure. Third, if you see your client has a destructive obsession with their case, let the mediator know. A good mediator has experience dealing with parties who are emotionally attached to their case. Alert the mediator in advance of the issue so they can look for opportunities to address it.

38.

What Happens If I Don't Settle?

"What will happen if I go to trial instead of settling my case?"

Mediation is often a day-long process with this question hanging over everyone's head. The answer is unknown, and that's what drives mediation. I recently came upon an article that addressed this question. In "Let's Not Make a Deal: An Empirical Study of Decision Making in Unsuccessful Settlement Negotiations," researchers dove into the statistics of unsuccessful settlement negotiations. The article is almost ten years old, but it still provides valuable insight.

The authors analyzed two thousand cases in California that went to trial or arbitration after unsuccessful settlement negotiations. In a nutshell, they found significant risks for both sides.[1]

When a plaintiff rejected a settlement offer and chose to go to trial, their result was—on average—$43,100 less than the last settlement offer. Further, the plaintiff's trial verdict was greater than their last settlement demand in only 24.3 percent of the cases.[2] In other words, the plaintiff usually does better at mediation than trial.

Defendants, however, should not be too quick to rejoice. Of those cases where plaintiffs did do better than their last settlement demand, the plaintiffs beat their last demand by an average of more than $1.1 million.[3] When the plaintiff does do better at trial, they *really* do better.

Most of you have heard me say that "a mediated settlement is almost always better for everyone." I think these statistics bear this out.

39.

You Can Agree to Disagree and Still Settle Your Case

Over Thanksgiving 2018, I finished a great book by historian Robert Dallek called *An Unfinished Life*. It is an insightful biography of the late John F. Kennedy. In his book, Dallek recounts a meeting between President Kennedy and Nikita Khrushchev regarding a potential arms control agreement. Khrushchev was intent on debating the merits of their respective positions. Kennedy listened for a long while, feeling that he could better negotiate with Khrushchev if he understood his interests.

After a while, however, Kennedy grew weary. He finally said, "Look, Mr. Chairman, you aren't going to make a communist out of me and I don't expect to make a capitalist out of you, so let's get down to business."[1]

I see something like this play out in mediation after mediation. Mediations tend to have a rhythm. The parties argue their positions early in the process. This is helpful. It's difficult to negotiate with someone without knowing their interests and their perceived strengths. Learning the other side's view allows you to make informed decisions when negotiating.

At some point, however, it is important to do what one mediator has called "the pivot."[2] This is the point where the parties talk less about their legal and factual positions and start talking about what a deal might look like. I call this the "agree-to-disagree" point. As I often remind people who mediate with me, you can agree to disagree and still settle your case.

If you're a negotiator who likes to "just get to the numbers" quickly, consider that hearing what the other side has to say in the early stages of the mediation might change your view of the case. You can learn weaknesses in your case that you didn't previously see. This can help you give better advice to your client.

By contrast, I've meditated with some people who won't talk seriously about terms until they think they have convinced the other side of their position. They grab hold of an argument and simply won't let go of it until the other side agrees with them. Remember that it's okay to disagree. You don't have to convince them you're right to resolve the case. As President Kennedy might say, "You'll never convince them to become a capitalist, so get down to business."

40.

It's Okay to Say Yes

One of the greatest impediments to settlement is a party's reluctance to say yes to the other party's offer. We have all been through this. We have negotiated for hours and hours. At the end of the day, one party says, "One million dollars, take it or leave it." The other side says, "Nine hundred ninety-five thousand, nine hundred ninety-five dollars: take it or leave it." And then the lines are drawn in the sand.

As a practical matter, no one is walking away. The difference between these two arbitrary bottom lines is negligible. As my accountant friends say, "It is immaterial." However, we are unable to take our advocacy hats off during the mediation, and impasse ensues.

There are various tricks used to overcome this imaginary impasse. We all know them. One party says, "Well, I'll take it, but they have to pay the mediator's fee." Alternatively, someone says, "We're not moving, but we'll listen to a mediator's proposal." The numbers I have used to illustrate the point are large. The smaller the numbers, the bigger the problem. A five-thousand-dollar difference is much more significant when we are dealing with five figures as opposed to seven. However, there are many times that everyone knows that a deal is on the table. Our pride gets in the way. We are unwilling to say yes to the adversary's proposal. This rarely blows up a settlement because someone eventually blinks. It does, however, create a lot of unnecessary gamesmanship at the end of a mediation. So one thing that your mediator wants you to know is that it is often in your client's best interest to just say yes.

Sometimes the best advocacy we can exhibit for our clients is simply to turn to them and say, "You know, we might be able to squeeze out another thousand—maybe even five—but we are going to burn up attorney time doing it. Let's just say yes to the offer on the table and go get a drink."

41.

Mediator's Proposals

For people who are supposed to be peacemakers, mediators can certainly squabble when they get together. I was at an ABA conference in Chicago a while back, and a colleague asked a group of mediators whether we ever made "mediator's proposals" in an effort to break an impasse. I said that, yes, I have made mediator's proposals as a last resort if negotiations are truly stalled. This opened a can of worms.

A couple of my colleagues argued that it was borderline heresy for a mediator to offer up a proposed settlement for the parties to consider. Doesn't that compromise our objectivity? Aren't we no longer being neutral?

"If you're proposing, you're not mediating," they told me.

I argued that mediator's proposals, while they should be rare, can be an effective way to find a resolution when the negotiations appear to have hit a dead end. I think history supports my view.

In 1979, President Carter had summoned the leaders of Israel and Egypt to Camp David in an effort to negotiate peace between their respective countries. Carter wanted to strictly be a facilitator. He believed—perhaps naively—that the two countries could work out their differences if they just talked to each other. This led nowhere. In fact, the parties were just getting more entrenched in their positions.

A few months earlier, Secretary of State Cyrus Vance had visited the late Professor Roger Fisher at Fisher's home in Martha's Vineyard. Fisher is the coauthor of the book *Getting to Yes*. He cofounded the Harvard Negotiation Project and pioneered dispute resolution as a field of academic study. Fisher argued to Vance that Carter should use the "One Document Approach" at Camp David. He said that Carter, as the mediator, should propose a settlement to both parties. This one document could then be the starting point, allowing the parties to work out the details of a settlement.[1]

At Camp David, President Carter drew upon this advice and made a "mediator's proposal." This broke the impasse. While significant negotiations were still necessary, the lasting peace between Israel and Egypt would not have occurred without a mediator's proposal.

Well, I've never been asked to mediate peace in the Middle East. I'm sure I never will. However, I have used mediator's proposals to help parties resolve many cases.

There are two things I believe everyone should remember when they ask for a mediator's proposal.

First, a mediator's proposal is not a case evaluation. It is nothing more than a mediator's guess regarding what might be acceptable to both sides. It's an educated guess, based on what we've heard all day. Still, it's just a guess.

Second, a mediator's proposal should only be used as a last resort to break an impasse. If the parties are still moving, then the process needs to play out. Mediator's proposals are a Hail Mary. You don't throw a Hail Mary if there's still time on the clock.

42.

Can I Lie to My Mediator about My Bottom Line?

I often say that, as a mediator, part of my job is to be lied to and smile about it. I make this comment because it adds some levity to a serious negotiation, which I think is helpful. I also say it because it's true.

The mediator is your voice in the other room. You communicate to your adversary though them. For this reason, lawyers have to be mindful of the duty of candor. You don't have to share your bad facts with the other side during a mediation. You don't have to disclose the case or the witness that will hurt you. You cannot, however, misrepresent a material fact through the mediator. ABA Model Rule of Professional Responsibility 4.1(a) says plainly, "In the course of representing a client, a lawyer may not knowingly make a false statement of material fact or law to a third person. . . ."[1]

Sounds pretty straightforward, right?

You can't ethically say "Bob will testify that my client is trustworthy" when you know that Bob will say your client is a pathological liar with the morals of any alley cat. Likewise, you can't ethically say that all of the case law is in your favor when you know darn well that the controlling case in your jurisdiction says you're toast.

But what about those times when you say, "My bottom is line is $150,000, and we won't settle for a penny less"? I have mediations every week where the plaintiff's lawyer says, "I'll never settle for less than X." The defense lawyer then says, "I'll never pay more than Y." Lo and behold, four hours later, the case settles somewhere between X and Y.

What happened? Have the lawyers violated Rule 4.1? It seems like they have certainly made false statements of material fact. Well, maybe not. Comment 2 to Rule 4.1 says that statements about "a party's intentions as to an acceptable settlement of a claim" are not statements of fact.[2] Who knew? In other words, you can lie through your teeth about your bottom line, and ABA Model Rule 4.1 accepts that this is just part of negotiations.

Of course, just because you can misstate your bottom line doesn't mean you *should* misstate your bottom line. This rule, however, does acknowledge the realities of mediation. I've often said that people do things at the end of a mediation that they are not willing to do at the beginning of a mediation. The process works. People learn things that force them to reevaluate their settlement positions. There is no shame in this. It's part of the value of a mediation.

I encourage lawyers and parties to be flexible in a mediation. Be willing to listen. Don't draw lines in the sand. When you do, however, remember that our ethical rules give you space to redraw those lines.

43.

You Should Always Leave a Mediation Disappointed

How should you feel after a mediation? According to the prevailing research, a successful mediator should leave a mediation with a settlement . . . but not altogether pleased.

Professor George B. Craver teaches negotiation at the George Washington University Law School. He is widely regarded as one of the leading researchers in the field of alternative dispute resolution. Professor Craver argues that lawyers should approach negotiations with "elevated, but realistic aspirations."[1]

Professor Craver explains, "There is a direct correlation between negotiator aspirations and bargaining outcomes—individuals who hope to obtain more advantageous results generally achieve better final terms than persons with modest expectations." Therefore, concludes Craver, aspiration levels should be "minimally realistic."[2]

There is a danger, however, where negotiators have aspirations that are too high. Craver explains, "Negotiators who formulate entirely unreasonable objectives are not likely to obtain their desired terms.

"Opposing parties," he continues, "will find their demands wholly unrealistic and move toward their nonsettlement alternatives." He concludes that "[i]t is thus crucial for bargainers to develop elevated expectations they can rationally defend."[3]

What does this mean? It means you should leave mediations disappointed. If you leave happy, your goals were probably too low. If you leave without a settlement, they were likely too high. When it comes to negotiation, disappointment is a *good* thing.

44.

Don't Aim for Perfection

I once had a client who told me he wanted a "one-hand-ed lawyer." He explained that all of his prior lawyers answered his questions by saying, "Well, on the one hand . . . but on the other hand. . . ."

Now, I suppose, I'm a two-handed mediator. I previously wrote about the importance of having "elevated expectations" when you enter into negotiations. As you get near the close of negotiations, however, we cannot let elevated expectations stand in the way of a deal.

I was reminded of this by a master negotiator, my wife. We recently made an offer on a new home. We had been passively looking for a while. This one had everything we were looking for. It was perfect. Except for one thing . . . the garage.

I have complained for years about not having enough room in my garage. I promised myself that the next house I bought would have a larger garage. This house fit our family perfectly, but the garage was the same size as the one in our current home. Maybe even a bit smaller.

I thought, I pondered, and I stressed about the garage. Should we have not made the offer? Will I ever have the garage I want? My wife finally said, "Look, we've found garages you liked, but you didn't like those other houses because of the office . . . or the yard . . . or the storage space . . . or. . . ." You get the picture. Then she looked at me and said, "Michael, no house is perfect."

Her comment hit me in the face. During the closing moments of mediations, I've often told parties, "Don't let the perfect be the enemy of the good." If you're close to a good deal, it's foolish to walk away because it's not perfect. A perfect result rarely comes in a courtroom. If it's unlikely to come in a courtroom, then it's unwise to hold out for it in a mediation.

We know that a negotiated deal is never perfect, but I find that parties lose sight of that in the heat of negotiations. Perhaps it's good to have a mediator (or spouse) there to remind us.

45.

Should We Tie Up the Loose Ends with Arbitration?

I used to co-host a series of podcasts for the ABA Section on Dispute Resolution. One of my first podcasts was an interview with Robert Margulies, a New Jersey lawyer who mediates international disputes. I was interested to learn that parties to an international dispute regularly agree to arbitrate any issues related to the implementation of the mediated settlement agreement. There are practical reasons for this. The New York Convention, which about 159 countries have signed, provides the mechanism to enforce arbitration awards. Without an arbitration clause, the parties in an international mediation might be left with a settlement agreement and no effective means to enforce it.[1]

This may also be a useful approach in commercial and employment disputes. At the end of a long and complex mediation, the parties typically sign a term sheet or memorandum of understanding that lists the primary elements of the deal. Sometimes, disputes arise when the parties later try to work out the details in the final agreement.

One way to prevent this is to steal a strategy from those who mediate international disputes. At the end of a difficult mediation, it is increasingly common for parties to include a clause in their mediation term sheet that says something like this: "In the event a dispute arises regarding the language of the final settlement agreement, the parties agree that Molly Mediator shall be the final arbitrator of those disputes and her decision will be binding."

This seems especially prevalent in complex commercial cases and class actions, where the parties want to exhaust all means to make sure a settlement does not fall apart.

I am neither an advocate nor a critic of this approach. Whether it's worth considering likely depends on the case. It may, however, be an option in difficult cases where the parties have reached a mediated settlement that they want to preserve at all costs.

46.

A Reasoned Mediator's Proposal

At the end of a mediation—when it's time to close—we mediators tend to have a number of tricks up our sleeve to try to push a deal across the finish line. You know many of them. The "hypothetical" offer. The bracket. The mediator's proposal. Sometimes it's just a good old-fashioned reality check.

Another option is a "reasoned mediator's proposal." Like a traditional mediator's proposal, this is where a mediator makes a proposal to settle the case, and each party has to independently respond with a yes or a no. Here's the twist: Instead of simply making the recommendation, the mediator also writes the reasoning behind the proposal and why he or she believes it is the appropriate resolution. The mediator may write one letter and send it to both parties. When I make a reasoned mediator's proposal, however, I usually send a separate letter or email to each party. I point out the concerns I would have if I were in that party's shoes and the reasons I believe *that party* should accept the mediator's proposal.

On the defendant's side, a reasoned mediator's proposal can be especially helpful if there is a board that must approve a settlement or a higher-ranking official that must sign off on it. In other words, a reasoned mediator's proposal can be helpful when you have to run it up the flagpole. On the other side, a reasoned mediator's proposal can give the plaintiff's counsel support for the advice that they are likely already giving their client.

47.

The Impact of a Pandemic on Mediation

In February 2020, my wife and I spent a long weekend in New York. We attended a show on Broadway, ate dinner at Patsy's, and shopped for books at the Strand. A global pandemic then seized the nation, and the "city that never sleeps"—New York—became strangely quiet.

As COVID-19 required mediations to shift almost exclusively to online platforms, I was astounded at how quickly the legal profession adapted. Like many of you, I have considered how this global pandemic will change the way we live, work, and play. I am especially interested in how the use of video-assisted mediations will impact the way we resolve disputes in the future. I want to share what I think we can learn from this experience.

Participants

In a recent mediation, I asked one of the lawyers for his thoughts about our online mediation. I was looking for his feedback on what went well and what could be done differently. His response surprised me. He said, "This case would not have settled if we had held the mediation in person."

He explained that his client's primary decision maker, who lived on the West Coast, would have never flown to Nashville for the mediation, regardless of whether there was a global pandemic. Conducting the mediation by Zoom, however, allowed his client to participate from start to finish. As a result, the client became invested in the process and was crucial to getting a deal done. I think lawyers are now more likely to urge key decision makers to participate by videoconference during the entire mediation rather than be "available by phone."

I also think litigants will be more comfortable with their opponents participating remotely. In years past, parties have said, "I'm not going to mediation unless the other side is there in person." We are learning that online mediations are extremely effective. Going forward, I think folks will be much more comfortable proceeding with a mediation if their opponent is participating remotely via videoconference.

Facilities

During the height of the COVID-19 pandemic, I mediated a case with multiple parties and five different law firms. It was conducted completely online, and we were able to get the case resolved. At the beginning of the mediation, I opened five different virtual rooms for the lawyers to meet separately with their respective clients. As the mediator, I moved between those virtual rooms, and the lawyers and parties met privately in various different groups, depending on the issue we were addressing at the moment.

If we had tried to do that in person, only a very large law firm with expansive facilities could have accommodated our conference room needs. Conducting the mediation online, however, was an efficient way to avoid taking up every conference room a law firm had available at the moment.

In very large multiparty cases, perhaps online mediation will develop as a way to manage these logistical challenges.

Cost Savings

When things return to something that resembles normal—and, as of 2022, we're still figuring out what that so-called "new normal" is—I am confident most mediations will return to in-person sessions. There are significant cost savings, however, that result from online mediations.

Consider the following possibility. One lawyer is in Los Angeles. One lawyer is in Chicago. The plaintiff has moved from Dallas to Philadelphia. The company is headquartered in Nashville. The case is pending in Dallas, where the plaintiff previously lived. The dispute is over a $150,000 contract. Does it make sense to fly everyone to Dallas (or somewhere else) for the mediation? Couldn't those resources be better allocated toward trying to reach a resolution? I think cases like this may make online mediation an attractive cost-effective option for parties in the future.

Looking Forward

When I was a young lawyer, one of the senior partners in my former law firm said, "A good lawyer never fails to take advantage of a crisis." To be sure, a pandemic is a crisis. It will be remembered as a difficult time in our nation's history. Perhaps, however, we can walk away with some valuable lessons.

48.

Let's Talk about Brackets

It seems that no lawyer is agnostic on the topic of "brackets." You either love them or hate them. Some folks love to propose a bracket early in a mediation. Others throw things at me when I convey a proposed bracket from the opposing party. My view is that brackets are a very effective negotiation tactic when parties understand how to use them.

Now, before I assume too much, let me be clear what I'm talking about when I use the term "bracket." A bracket—or a "band" as they're called in some parts of the country—is just a conditional offer. The plaintiff might say, "I'll offer $700,000 *conditioned* on you countering with an offer of $400,000." In response, the defendant might say, "I can't do that, but I'll offer $300,000 *conditioned* on you responding with an offer of $600,000."

In 2021, Lawrence M. Watson Jr. published an article in the *American Journal of Mediation* titled "Bracketology: The Art and Science of Bracket Negotiations." In researching the article, he conducted a survey of leading mediators and found the following:

- 97.5 percent of mediators have used brackets in their mediation practice.

- Only 2.5 percent have not.

- 62.5 percent of mediators say they "frequently" or "almost always" see brackets used in mediations.

- 37.5 percent of mediators say they "infrequently" or "rarely" see brackets.

- 55 percent of mediators say brackets are most frequently proposed late in negotiations.

- 45 percent of mediators say they are used "anytime."

- When brackets are proposed, 70 percent of mediators say the parties "almost always" focus on the midpoints.[1]

Why are brackets a useful tool in negotiations? Watson argues that brackets eliminate "the fear of flying" in mediation. He explains, "In single number negotiations, as initial offers and demands are asserted, the parties will often react with an emotional distrust for the side's position."[2] He writes that "'Fear of Flying' in settlement negotiations [is the] fear that the opposition will not reciprocate to a reasonable settlement overture in an equally reasonable manner. This concern often inhibits a party from making a meaningful [move] toward settlement in the first place."[3]

In other words, brackets protect you when you want to make a significant move and generate some momentum, but you're not sure the opponent will reciprocate.

In my experience, the best negotiators almost always use brackets. They understand how to send a signal with a bracket that they can't send by simply proposing a number. They also understand that when they receive a bracket, they are getting a much better indication of their opponent's ultimate settlement position than they would get in a single-number negotiation.

I'll close with this anecdote. I recently mediated a very difficult case between two lawyers who knew each other very well. Each side was making very incremental moves, and both clients were growing frustrated. I pulled the lawyers into the room with me and said, "Look, I can stay here all night, but both of your clients are getting fed up with the pace of your negotiations." One of the lawyers looked at me and said, "When everyone is pissed off . . . it's time to move to brackets."

The case settled an hour later.

49.

Consider a "Structured Mediation"

Many of you have heard me say that mediations occur in three phases: (1) positioning, (2) bargaining, and (3) closing.

Positioning is where the parties exchange information, legal arguments, and factual perspectives. In other words, that's when they argue their case. During the positioning phase, the parties will also usually exchange initial offers. However, the messages are often more important than the offers when the parties are still positioning.

When the parties move to the bargaining phase, they get down to brass tacks. That's when offers and counteroffers start flying back and forth.

The final stage is closing. That's when everyone gets mad, and we usually get a deal.

One of the most frustrating things for lawyers and parties is when there is disagreement about when to pivot from one stage to another. One party might say, "I'm tired of talking about my legal position. I've told them all I'm going to tell them. Let's start talking numbers." Their opposing party might respond, "Well, I'm not talking numbers until I'm finished explaining my position."

This can be extremely frustrating to both sides and significantly impede the negotiation. One way to manage this problem is to "structure" the mediation. I have had a number of cases recently where lawyers have called me in advance of the mediation and have already agreed in advance to a structure for the mediation. Here are two examples.

In one significant commercial case, the parties agreed that I would set aside one day about a week prior to the mediation to hear their views of the case. I met with the plaintiff's counsel in the morning, who shared their evidence, legal theories, and opening offer. After lunch, I went to the defense counsel's office. I shared what I had heard that morning from the plaintiff's counsel. The defense counsel then shared their rebuttal and their response to the opening demand. Finally, I met again briefly with plaintiff's counsel to share both the defendant's first offer and their rebuttal. The second day of mediation was scheduled a week later and would consist of bargaining. The parties used the time between the first session and second session to meet their clients' executives to see if their positions had changed before they entered the bargaining phase. I have to give the lawyers all the credit. This wasn't my idea. They brought it to me, and it worked very well.

In a recent class action, the lawyers agreed to something similar. They wanted me to meet with each of their expert witnesses in advance of the mediation. I then shared with the other side what I had heard from the opposing party's expert. The lawyers then came to the mediation the following day well informed as to the other party's position and ready to bargain. This approach works best on larger cases with a lot of moving parts. It allows the lawyers and the clients to come to the mediation well prepared and informed of the opposing party's position.

If you have a case that looks like it will be a bear to mediate, you might consider exploring this structured approach with your adversary.

50.

Great Negotiators Know When to Fold

James Baker is widely regarded as one of the best negotiators in American history. A Texas lawyer, Baker leveraged his friendship with a young George H.W. Bush to positions as White House chief of staff, treasury secretary, and secretary of state.

His reputation as a dealmaker in Washington is legendary. One of his most significant negotiations involved the United States' first free-trade agreement with Canada, a deal upon which NAFTA would later be based. The deal, however, almost fell apart.

The US and Canada had long hoped to reach a comprehensive free-trade agreement, but the deal had remained elusive. President Ronald Reagan asked Baker to take the lead in negotiations, and after multiple rounds of talks, a deal was within reach. However, there remained one sticking point.

The Canadians held out for a dispute resolution process as part of the final agreement. The Americans viewed this as a compromise of their sovereignty and refused to agree. In the end, Baker reluctantly caved on the issue. In a recently published biography, *The Man Who Ran Washington: The Life and Times of James A. Baker III*, the authors recount this exchange between Baker and Canadian Prime Minister Brian Mulroney:

> "Well, I'll tell you, Jim, if that's the case I'm going to call President Reagan," Mulroney said. "He's at Camp David and I just have one question to ask him."
>
> "What's that?"
>
> "I'm going to say, 'Now, Ron, how is it that the United States can agree to a nuclear reduction deal with their worst enemy, the Soviet Union, and they can't agree to a free trade agreement with their best friend, the Canadians?'"
>
> Baker did not like the sound of that. "Prime Minister, can you give me twenty minutes?"
>
> "Sure."
>
> Finally, at 9 p.m., Baker burst into the office where [the Canadian negotiator] had been waiting and tossed a piece of paper on the table.
>
> "All right," he said, "you can have your goddamn dispute settlement mechanism."[1]

Baker had caved. One of America's great negotiators had capitulated.

Here's the thing. Few remember that Baker folded. Rather, history remembers Baker as the guy who got the deal when previous American negotiators had failed.

In mediations, we often see lawyers and clients draw lines in the sand over collateral issues. When that happens, it's important to ask ourselves, "Is this important enough to blow up the whole deal?" It's usually not.

Let's take a lesson from James Baker. Before you lose a deal, make sure the issue is a hill you're willing to die on.

51.

You're Not the Only One Who's Glad the Case Settled

When the parties walk away from a successful mediation, they usually experience a myriad of emotions. The plaintiff is happy to look forward to a recovery but probably disappointed that they are not getting more money. The defendant is mad about the amount of money they are going to pay but relieved to have avoided the expense and uncertainty of continued litigation. More than anything else, the parties are probably just glad it's over.

The parties may not appreciate that they are not the only people who are glad it's over. The judge is too. And I can prove it.

On July 19, 2011, Judge Martin J. Sheehan, a state court trial judge in Kentucky, entered the following

Order in the case of *Barbara Kissel v. Schwartz & Maines & Ruby Co, LPA, et al.*:

> The herein matter having been scheduled for trial by jury commencing July 13, 2011, and numerous pre-trial motions having yet to be decided and remaining under submission;
>
> And the parties having informed the Court that the herein matter has been settled amicably (The Court uses the work "amicably" loosely) and that there is no need for a Court ruling on the remaining motions and also that there is no need for a trial;
>
> And such news of an amicable settlement having made this Court happier than a tick on a fat dog because it is otherwise busier than a one legged cat in a sand box and; quite frankly, would have rather jumped naked off of a twelve foot step ladder into a five gallon bucket of porcupines than have presided over a two week trial of the herein dispute, a trial which, no doubt, would have made the jury more confused than a hungry baby in a topless bar and made the parties and their attorneys madder than mosquitoes in a mannequin factory;
>
> **IT IS THEREFORE ORDERED ADJUDGED AND DECREED** by the court as follows:
>
> - The jury trial scheduled for July 13, 2011, is hereby CANCELED.
>
> - Any and all pending motions will remain under submission pending the filing of an Agreed

Judgment, Agreed Entry of Dismissal, or other pleadings consistent with the parties' settlement.

- The copies of various correspondence submitted for in camera review by the Defendant, SMRS, shall be sealed by the Clerk until further order of the Court.

- The Clerk shall engage the services of a structural engineer to ascertain if the return of this file to the Clerk's office will exceed the maximum structural load of the floors of said office.

Dated this 19th day of July 2011

Martin J. Sheehan
Kenton Circuit Judge[1]

Epilogue

So, You Want to Be a Mediator?

"Can I take you to lunch?"

I get that question a lot. Lawyers frequently reach out to me for lunch meetings so they can pick my brain about breaking into the mediation game. I'm always glad to talk with folks who are interested in transitioning from an advocate to a neutral. The problem, however, is that mediators don't get lunch breaks. We're always trying to resolve a dispute while other lawyers are eating a grilled chicken salad at the deli down the street. In light of this, I decided to devote the final pages of this book to the questions I am most often asked by aspiring mediators. In other words, this is our lunch date.

Is It Better than Practicing Law?

When lawyers ask me about being a mediator, it usually means they're tired. Tired of discovery disputes.

Tired of motion practice. Tired of difficult opposing counsel. Tired of temperamental judges. And, yes, tired of demanding clients. I get it. I've been there. When lawyers look at transitioning from being an advocate to being a neutral, they are often burned out on the practice of law but want to stay engaged in the legal field. I don't know if being a mediator is better than being a practicing lawyer, but it is certainly different. From my perspective, here are the pros and cons.

Folks who don't make it as a mediator often are surprised by how little control mediators have over their days. When I was a practicing litigator, I had much more flexibility to attend to things during the day. If I needed to pick up a sick child at school and my spouse couldn't, it was usually no problem. If I wasn't in a deposition or at court, I could drop what I was doing and pick it up later. Mediators can't do that.

My colleague and mentor, Allen Blair, says that his wife calls herself a "mediation widow." When a mediator leaves home in the morning, they may be finished at four o'clock in the afternoon, or they may be finished at midnight. Regardless, there's no tearing yourself away for a quick errand over lunch. This is often a shock to lawyers who are accustomed to significant flexibility.

I think that retired lawyers and judges often see mediation as a good second act. Maybe it's viewed as a way to ease into retirement. Over the last twenty years, I've seen fewer and fewer retired judges successfully launching second careers as mediators. I think this is due in part to how surprised they are by the lack of control they have over their day-to-day schedule.

Well, all *that* was pessimistic.

Now the good news.

While mediation is much more work than folks appreciate, it is also far less stressful than the day-to-day grind of litigation. Like most trial lawyers, I've spent my fair share of sleepless nights, worrying about discovery deadlines, important hearings, and pending trials. Mediators don't do that. We put in a hard day of work, trying to help you resolve your cases. The vast majority of times, we are able to help you settle your cases. On the rare occasions we not successful, we send our bill and close our file. Yes, we'll follow up. Yes, we'll try to stay engaged. And absolutely, we'll get involved again if the parties think it would be helpful. Mostly, however, mediators have a short memory, because we have someone else's dispute we have to tackle tomorrow.

If mediation is something you believe will be easy, I have to disavow you of that. My wife will tell you I work more hours as a mediator than I ever did as a lawyer. If your goal is to "slow down," I think most judges and lawyers who have tried that have not fared well. On the other hand, in my experience, being a mediator is not stressful. It's hard work, a valuable service, and extremely rewarding. But I sleep pretty darn well at night.

What Does It Take to Be a Successful Mediator?

I get this question a lot, but it's not really the question people want to ask. What they really want to ask is, "Can I be a success as a mediator?"

What does it take to make it as a mediator? This is a question that even successful mediators wrestle with.

First off, let's just acknowledge that mediation is a competitive field. There are far more trained mediators than people who are actually making a living doing it. When I was first breaking in as a full-time mediator, one experienced neutral told me, "It's tough out there . . . every sonofabitch and his brother want to do this."

A few years ago, I co-taught a class for new mediators with Peter Robinson, who was then director of the Straus Institute for Dispute Resolution at Pepperdine University. Few people in the country have trained more mediators than Peter. He is simply one of the best teachers of mediation I've ever seen. Over coffee, Peter and I discussed the difficulty aspiring mediators face.

Peter, who lives in Southern California, believes that being a professional mediator is much like being a professional actor. Those who are successful are richly rewarded. Others are waiting tables as they struggle to make it.

I had a similar conversation with Parag Shah, chief operating officer of Miles Mediation and Arbitration Service. Parag believes being a mediator is like being a basketball player. Some folks have the combination of talent and work ethic—like LeBron James—to rise to the top. Others have less natural talent and may never charge the top rates, but through hard work and good training, they can still make a good living as a neutral.

I think both Peter and Parag make good points, and it's not all that different from the experience of trial lawyers. Some attorneys are just not comfortable in a courtroom. Others are solid trial lawyers but have to work at it. Still others can make a jury weep by changing the inflection in their voices.

I can't help but think life experiences also play a significant role. I have very few skills in life. I'm worthless as a handyman. I can't change a tire, nor can I change the oil in my car. Heck, I'm not even sure I know how to check the oil in my current car. But I've found I have a talent in talking with people and persuading them to resolve their disputes. I think it has a lot to do with my background.

My father died in a car accident when I was seventeen days old. My mother worked in a garment factory, sewing legs on pants so that I would have clothes on my back, a roof over my head, and food on my table. When I was young, our house didn't have an indoor toilet. We had to go use the outhouse. Because of the grace of the good Lord and a little talent, I was able to get a good education and have a successful legal career. One of my former associates—whose father is a successful corporate lawyer—said that I'm the only lawyer she knows who is just as comfortable on a factory floor as I am at the country club. Through my circumstances, I've learned to communicate with people from all walks of life. At the end of the day, I think this has been the secret to my success as a mediator.

Every aspiring mediator has to take stock of themselves. Am I willing to work at my craft? Do I have emotional intelligence? Can I earn people's trust? Am I comfortable talking to folks from vastly different walks of life? Are people comfortable around me? Can I have a difficult conversation in a diplomatic way? Can I put people at ease? Can I simplify difficult concepts so a lay person can understand them? Am I persuasive? Am I patient? These are the questions you should wrestle with as you decide whether to take the plunge as a mediator.

What Should a Young Lawyer Do If He or She Wants to Be a Mediator Down the Road?

I often joke that I decided to be a mediator when I realized that Scripture says "blessed are the peacemakers"[1] and not "blessed are the litigators." The truth, however, is that I wanted to be a mediator since the day I graduated from law school.

When I was a summer clerk at a law firm, I attended a sexual harassment mediation with one of the partners. The whole process fascinated me. I then took a mediation course in law school from an adjunct professor who would go on to be a trusted mentor. I scored the highest grade in the class and later went to work at the law firm where my mediation professor was a partner. Even as a young associate, I knew I wanted to eventually work my way into a mediation practice. If you are a young lawyer and like-minded, here are a few tips.

First of all, you have to be an excellent lawyer. People don't become successful mediators if they have a reputation of being lazy or mediocre lawyers.

Second, find a way to get in a courtroom. I developed a full-time mediation practice much earlier than I expected. I think part of the reason is that I spent much of my career in a small firm that allowed me to get to court more often than many of my peers. This allowed me to build credibility with more senior lawyers who would eventually hire me to mediate their cases.

Third, don't be a jackass. This is probably more important than anything else when first breaking in as a mediator. Your opposing counsel and co-counsel are your future mediation clients. Avoid discovery disputes if at all possible. Grant extensions to your opponent. Compliment your opponent when they write a good brief. Be gracious when you lose. Be humble when you win. (I always wanted my opposing counsel to view me as a formidable adversary but not an enemy. Over the years, my co-counsel and adversaries became friends. And then they became my mediation clients.)

Fourth, invest in good mediation training. Let's talk about that now.

Where Should I Go for My Mediation Training?

I've said that a good mediator is a combination of hard work, talent, and good training. It's important not to overlook the education component. The greatest trial lawyer in the world is worthless if she doesn't know the Rules of Evidence. Mediators are no different. There are certain skills that must be learned, practiced, and then perfected. In other words, good training is crucial.

There are several excellent providers. If you want to go all in, you might consider an LL.M. in Dispute Resolution. The University of Missouri has the oldest such LL.M. program in the country. Founded by Professor Leonard Riskin, the Mizzou LL.M. has been a pioneer in dispute resolution education. They now even offer their LL.M. program by distance education. As an alum, however, I suppose I'm a bit biased. Pepperdine University also offers an excellent LL.M. program in dispute resolution. They, too, offer an online option.

For a more traditional short-term program, there are three providers I most often recommend. The Straus Institute at Pepperdine University regularly offers a forty-hour course called "Mediating the Litigated Case," which receives excellent reviews.

The Program on Negotiation at Harvard also produces two well-respected multiday mediation programs. "Mediating Disputes" is a five-day foundation class. The other, "The Harvard Negotiation Master Class," is a three-day program for more advanced practitioners. The Harvard program was founded by Professor Roger Fisher, who co-authored the influential book *Getting to Yes*.

In Nashville, the Institute for Conflict Management at Lipscomb University hosts several well-received trainings annually. The Lipscomb program is held over the course of two weekends to accommodate the schedule of busy lawyers.

Can I Be a Full-Time Mediator and Stay at My Law Firm?

Probably not. There have certainly been some very successful mediators who have worked out acceptable arrangements with their law firms. Being at a law firm while you are growing your mediation practice also provides security. Building a mediation practice is a marathon, not a sprint. It takes time. I maintained a full-time litigation practice for several years while building my mediation practice. At some point, however, I just don't think a traditional law firm is an ideal platform for a robust mediation practice. In my view, few mediators can take their practice to the highest level while remaining a member of a traditional law firm. There are at least two reasons for this.

The first reason is obvious: conflicts. When I was a partner at an Am Law 200 firm, I was constantly trying to navigate conflicts in my mediation practice. My firm was wonderful and supportive of my growing ADR practice. They also seemed to represent everyone in town. If folks have decided to hire you as a mediator, they have already decided you're honest and a person of character. If the conflict can be waived, the parties are generally willing to waive it. But it's still a pain.

The second reason is more problematic. The economics of a law practice and a mediation practice are vastly different. A law firm generally requires associates, paralegals, staff, escrow accounts, Westlaw subscriptions, and a marketing budget. A mediation practice requires a cell phone and a tank of gas.

A law firm carries significant overhead, but it makes money from leverage.[2] A mediation practice has no leverage, but it makes money because there's no overhead. As a mediator, very little of my personal billing is used to cover overhead. That's one of the great things about the business of mediation. It also makes it very difficult for a successful mediator to remain in his or her law firm.

Can I Mediate Part Time While Maintaining an Active Law Practice?

In my view, mediators can maintain active law practices for a period of time while building a mediation practice. At some point, however, I think you have to decide where you're going to concentrate your efforts. As I said previously, a law firm is a great platform to grow a mediation practice because it provides some financial stability as you build your mediation book of business. I don't think this is workable over the long haul.

I love to play tennis. I play every chance I get, but I'm essentially a weekend warrior. I have friends who play almost every day. They're better than I am, and part of the reason is they spend more time on the tennis court than I do.

The same is true for mediators. Those who mediate a case almost every day are going to develop skills that folks who mediate a handful of cases per month just can't develop. It's not because full-time mediators are smarter or more talented. It's just that mediating and litigating require two different skill sets. In my experience, it's very difficult to switch back and forth between the two.

Another reason that I found it difficult to split time between being a mediator and a practicing lawyer simply relates to the nature of the legal profession. When you hire me to mediate a case, you're paying for my full attention for the whole day. As a lawyer, I had clients who had urgent matters arise that required my immediate attention. If a mediation client was paying me to devote myself to them all day, and a litigation client had an urgent matter and needed me on an unexpected conference call at one thirty, I never found that I could balance those two obligations.

How Should I Get Started?

Volunteer your time. There are numerous pro bono mediation programs. I think that's where every mediator should start. First, it will give you a good sense of whether you will enjoy it. More than a few lawyers have thought they wanted to be a mediator, only to find out they didn't enjoy it like they thought they would. Second, if you find you enjoy the role of a neutral, getting a few pro bono mediations under your belt will help you hone your skills and create a track record.

One of my first breaks as a mediator came as a result of pro bono program launched by the military. Guard and reservists were returning from Iraq and getting into disputes with their employers over whether they were entitled to re-employment under a federal law called the Uniform Services Employment and Reemployment Rights Act (USERRA). As a volunteer ombudsman, I served as a mediator in these disputes. I got some real-world experience, and the local newspaper ran a short article about my volunteer work. The publicity was nice, but the experience also convinced me that I really was cut out for this work.

There are programs like this everywhere, and I think those are a great place for aspiring mediators to start. You might be surprised where a quick call to the local bar association or clerk of court will lead you.

Any Final Thoughts for Aspiring Mediators?

Building a mediation practice is a marathon; it's not a sprint. The only way to grow an ADR practice is to do it gradually. The good news is that being a mediator is a meritocracy. If you're good at it, you'll be successful. Your first few cases are the hardest ones to get. Once you get those, you're on your way. If you do a good job, the lawyers who hired you will always come back, and they'll bring different opposing counsel next time. Slowly . . . but surely . . . word will get around.

Acknowledgments

I'm not sure I've ever had an original thought in my life. Almost everything I know about negotiation and mediation I've learned from others. Allen Blair, Hayden Lait, Mark Travis, Jim Kay, Peter Robinson, Paul Ladehoff, Hunter Hughes, and Tracy Shaw are just a few of the many mediators from whom I have drawn ideas and techniques. I have tried to attribute credit where I could, but I have certainly borrowed from folks without realizing it. I can only repay them by inviting young mediators to observe my techniques, claim them as their own, and improve upon them.

I am indebted to the faculty at the University of Missouri Law School's Center for the Study of Dispute Resolution. My academic work at Mizzou has provided a theoretical framework for my mediation practice. As I often told Professor Paul Ladehoff, my LL.M. advisor, Mizzou helped me understand the "why" behind the "how." The dispute resolution faculty at Mizzou Law deserves significant credit for shaping my thoughts on mediation and negotiation.

Cara Stegall provided the administrative assistance that brought this book to completion. Her professionalism and friendship cannot be overstated.

Caraline Rickard is an outstanding young attorney with a brilliant legal mind. She's also a dear friend who was kind enough to read a draft of this manuscript and offer valuable thoughts and edits.

A special word of thanks goes to my editor, Gail Fallen, whose talent and good humor kept me on task and greatly improved this book. Any errors, however, are mine alone.

Prior to becoming a full-time neutral, I was blessed to work at some excellent law firms that greatly influenced my mediation practice. I hesitate to mention names because I'll forget someone, but I hope you know who you are. I have the best former law partners, associates, paralegals, and legal assistants. Your friendship still means the world to me.

The lawyers who have hired me to mediate their cases merit special thanks. One veteran mediator told me that "this is a relationship business." He was right. I've had the privilege of working with the most talented lawyers in the country. Most have become friends. I cannot express my appreciation for the trust they have placed in me over the years.

Most important, I have to acknowledge my family. Alex Haley was fond of saying, "If you see a turtle on a fence post, you can bet he had some help getting there."[1]

Well, I'm the turtle on the fence post. My father died when I was seventeen days old. My mother, Linda, sacrificed immeasurably for me. My wife, Heather, is the most remarkable life partner imaginable. My in-laws, Cecil and Babs, welcomed me into their family twenty-five years ago and accepted me as one of their own. My sons, Preston and Carlisle, are my pride and joy. Whatever measure of success I may have is because of these people. I stand on their shoulders, and this book would not have been possible without their support.

Notes

Chapter 1

1. Abraham Lincoln, "Notes for a Law Lecture," in *The Collected Works of Abraham Lincoln,* Vol. 2, ed. Roy P. Basler (New Brunswick, NJ: Rutgers University Press, 1953), 81.

Chapter 3

2. Nancy H. Rogers, Robert C. Bordone, Frank E. A. Sander, and Craig A. McEwen, *Designing Systems and Processes for Managing Disputes,* 2nd ed. (New York: Wolters Kluwer, 2019), 222.

Chapter 4

1. Pepperdine University School of Law, "Straus Institute Conversation Series Featuring Ken Feinberg," 1:33:31, December 8, 2011, www.youtube.com/watch?v=aTJTjPL54LU.

2. Pepperdine, "Ken Feinberg."

Chapter 5

1. Brian Farkas and Donna Erez-Navot, "First Impressions: Drafting Effective Mediation Statements," *Lewis & Clark Law Review* 22, no. 1 (2018): 167–69.

2. Farkas and Erez-Navot, "First Impressions," 168.

3. Farkas and Erez-Navot, 177.

4. Farkas and Erez-Navot, 169.

5. Farkas and Erez-Navot, 169–70.

6. Farkas and Erez-Navot, 170.

Chapter 12

1. Ifat Maoz, Andrew Ward, Michael Katz, and Lee Ross, "Reactive Devaluation of an 'Israeli' vs. 'Palestinian' Peace Proposal," *Journal of Conflict Resolution* 46, no. 4 (August 2002): 515–46. https://doi.org/10.1177/00220027020460 04003.

Chapter 17

1. Russell Korobkin, *Negotiation: Theory and Strategy,* 2nd ed. (New York: Wolters Kluwer, 2009), 176.

2. Korobkin, *Negotiation*.

Chapter 18

1. Hon. Gerald E. Rosen (Ret.), "The Detroit Bankruptcy: The Power of Mediation" (presentation, American Bar Association Section on Dispute Resolution Spring Conference, Washington Hilton, Washington, DC, April 5, 2018).

2. Rosen, "Detroit Bankruptcy."

3. Rosen.

Chapter 19

1. Chapter 19 relies heavily on my graduate work at Vanderbilt University, specifically the Middle Eastern politics class taught by Professor Katherine Blue Carroll as part of the university's MLAS program. For additional reading on this topic, see Katherine Blue Carroll, "Tribal

Law and Reconciliation in the New Iraq," *Middle East Journal* 65, no. 1 (Winter 2011): 11–29.

Chapter 20

1. Lewis R. Donelson III, *Lewie* (Memphis: Rhodes College, 2012), 205–06.

2. Donelson, *Lewie*, 210.

Chapter 22

1. See Katie Shonk, "Body Language in the Negotiation Process and the Impact of Gender at the Bargaining Table," *Harvard Negotiation Project* (blog), September 24, 2019, www.pon.harvard.edu/daily/leadership-skills-daily/women-and-negotiation-permission-to-skip-the-chit-chat/.

2. Charles B. Craver, "What Makes A Great Legal Negotiator?" *Loyola Law Review* 56 (2010): 337, available at http://www2.hawaii.edu/~barkai/HO/What%20 Makes%20A%20Great%20Legal%20Negotiator%20-%20 Craver.pdf (last visited April 8, 2022).

Chapter 23

1. *Endgame*, directed by Pete Travis (London, UK: Target Entertainment, 2009).

Chapter 24

1. Roselle L. Wissler, "Court-Connected Mediation in General Civil Cases: What We Know from Empirical Research," *Ohio State Journal on Dispute Resolution* 17 (2002): 641, 671.

2. Wissler, "Court-Connected Mediation."

Chapter 25

1. V. Hale Starr, "The Simple Math of Negotiating," *The Trial Lawyer* 22, no. 5 (January–February 1999): 7–8 .

2. Chris Guthrie and Dan Orr, "Anchoring, Information, Expertise, and Negotiation: New Insights from Meta-Analysis," *Ohio State Journal on Dispute Resolution* 21 (2006): 597.

3. Deepak Mahortra and Max Bazerman, *Negotiation Genius: How to Overcome Obstacles and Achieve Brilliant Results at the Bargaining Table and Beyond* (New York: Bantam Dell, 2008), 35.

Chapter 26

1. Rogers, Bordone, Sander, and McEwen, *Designing Systems*, 74.

2. Tom R. Tyler, "Governing Pluralistic Societies," *Law and Contemporary Problems* 72 (Spring 2009): 187–92.

Chapter 29

1. Leonard L. Riskin, "Understanding Mediators' Orientations, Strategies, and Techniques: A Grid for the Perplexed," *Harvard Negotiation Law Review* 1, no. 7 (1996), available at https://scholarship.law.ufl.edu/cgi/viewcontent.cgi?referer=&httpsredir=1&article=1684&context=facultypub.

2. Riskin, "Understanding Mediators' Orientations."

3. Riskin.

Chapter 30

1. Riskin, "Understanding Mediators' Orientations."

2. Riskin.

3. Riskin.

Chapter 33

1. Greg Parent, "Don't Let Mediation Become Routine," (guest lecture, Alternative Dispute Resolution, Belmont University College of Law, Nashville, Tennessee, 2021).

Chapter 37

1. Kristy Hanstad, "Dealing with Difficult People and Negotiation: When Should You Give Up the Fight?" *Harvard Law School Program on Negotiation Daily Blog* (February 22, 2022), available at https://www.pon.harvard.edu/daily/dealing-with-difficult-people-daily/dealing-with-difficult-people-and-negotiation-when-should-you-give-up-the-fight/?fbclid=I-wAR1ws4RxJnTT Q6p2d0cSn96AlEVLM-2A_YtUu9ZVHta6gU9KzG1TYTgtOdw (last visited May 2, 2022).

2. Hanstad, "Difficult People."

3. Hanstad.

Chapter 38

1. Randall L. Kiser, Martin A. Asher, and Blakeley B. McShane, "Let's Not Make a Deal: An Empirical Study of Decision Making in Unsuccessful Settlement Negotiations," *Journal of Empirical Legal Studies* 5, no. 3 (September 2008): 551–91.

2. Kiser, Asher, and McShane, "Let's Not Make a Deal."

3. Kiser, Asher, and McShane.

Chapter 39

1. Robert Dallek, *An Unfinished Life: John F. Kennedy, 1917-1963* (New York: Little, Brown, and Company, 2003), 410.

2. Gene Moscovitch, "The Pivot," *International Academy of Mediators* (blog), October 27, 2015, iamed.org/blog/iam-blog-gene-moscovitch/.

Chapter 41

1. Lawrence Wright, *Thirteen Days in September: Carter, Begin, and Sadat at Camp David* (New York: Simon and Schuster, 2014), 61.

Chapter 42

1. American Bar Association [ABA], Center for Professional Responsibility, "Rule 4.1: Truthfulness in Statements to Others," 2019, available at https://www.americanbar.org/groups/professional_responsibility/publications/model_rules_of_professional_conduct/rule_4_1_truthfulness_in_statements_to_others/.

2. ABA, Center for Professional Responsibility, "Rule 4.1," cmt. 2.

Chapter 43

1. Craver, "What Makes a Great Legal Negotiator?" *Loyola Law Review,* 2010.

2. Craver.

3. Craver.

Chapter 45

1. Robert Margulies, "Conversation About the Enforcement of Mediation Agreements Across Borders," *Resolutions, A Podcast of the American Bar Association Section on Dispute Resolution,* March 21, 2019, www.americanbar.org/groups/dispute_resolution/resources/resolutions-a-podcast-about-dispute-resolution-and-prevention/resolutions-podcast-robert-margulies/.

Chapter 48

1. Lawrence M. Watson Jr., "Bracketology: The Art and Science of Bracket Negotiations," *The American Journal of Mediation* 13 (2021).

2. Watson, "Bracketology."

3. Watson.

Chapter 50

1. Peter Baker and Susan Glasser, *The Man Who Ran Washington: The Life and Times of James A. Baker III* (New York: Doubleday, 2020), 282–83.

Chapter 51

1. Barbara Kissel v. Schwartz & Maines & Ruby Co, LPA, et al., Case No. 09-CI-00165 (Kenton [KY] Circuit Court, July 19, 2011), available at www.legaljuice.com/files/2013/09/OrderKentonCourt.pdf.

Epilogue

1. Matt. 5:9 New International Version.

2. When we say "leverage" in the context of a law firm, we generally mean the ability of some partners ("rainmak-

ers") to originate legal work and funnel it down to other billers (less senior partners, associates, and paralegals).

Acknowledgments

1. Stephen Boyd, "The Turtle on the Fence Post," *Public Speaking Tips* (blog), October 21, 2011, speaking-tips.com/Articles/The-Turtle-On-The-Fence-Post.aspx.